'This book exposes the great nee[...] gentleness and tenderness whilst a[...] desperate need of a better vision of G[...] us to step away from the things we hi[...] to be vulnerable before God once again. She reminds us that His gaze may be penetrating but He is never dismissive or uncaring. Her words ooze with hopefulness. Hopefulness grounded in the beauty of a God who lovingly crafted each one of us for intimacy and longingly searches for us. She paints a picture of God with her words which reverberates deeply within the human heart. We see in her words a Father who yearns for intimacy with us and who will stop at nothing to pursue us. Her invitation to vulnerability is offered out of a life that has learned the beauty and the transformation that flows from allowing God into every area of our lives. This book moved me, challenged me, inspired me and encouraged me, but most of all it reminded me that God is deeply, deeply committed to His people and longs to hear us say, "Yes" to His staggering invitation to intimacy. I cannot commend it highly enough.'

Malcolm Duncan, author, Senior Pastor of Gold Hill Baptist Church and Chairman of Spring Harvest Planning Group

'In *Losing the fig leaf* Nicki Copeland brings together her personal experiences of dealing with low self-esteem and lack of confidence, and her personal revelation of the knowledge of a deep, healing love of God experienced through the study of Scripture, prayer, and listening to the Spirit. This is a scrupulously honest book, full of spiritual insight and wise advice. It will speak to many who are longing to know and understand more of their worth in God's eyes.'

Dr Lucy Peppiatt, Principal, Westminster Theological Centre

'A beautifully honest and biblical exploration of a journey out of hiding into fullness of life as a child of God. Within these pages Nicki offers her reader a compelling invitation to step away from the things they hide behind and discover the inheritance that we each have in God.'

Lindsay Melluish, pastor, therapist, speaker, author

'Nicki's powerful vulnerability and insightful scriptural undergirding speaks so relevantly to us today. Her story, woven through the pages, enables us to be real with ourselves, find a way to lose the fig leaf and to live in the fullness of Christ's freedom.'
Anne Calver, Baptist minister and author

'This is a fascinating book. It takes the ancient story of Adam and Eve and shows how relevant it is for today. Nicki names the "fig leaves" we hide behind and brings fresh insight to the struggles we experience in living the abundant life Jesus offers.'
Lin Button, author and founder of Healing Prayer School

'Nicki Copeland's careful exegesis on Genesis 1–3 and her understanding of its place within the wider biblical narrative of God's redemption and restoration forms the basis of a book that is rich in applied theology. Personal and practical, thoughtful and thought-provoking, *Losing the fig leaf* shares the lessons learned from a life lived humbly, honestly and purposefully, in relationship with the God of salvation.'
Freddy Hedley, Fountain School of Theology and author of The God of Page One

'Nicki Copeland explores the ways we hide with a gentle, authentic manner. Reading her book is like having a loving friend lead you into God's presence so you can become who He created you to be. John 1:12 in *The Message* describes the God-begotten as those who believed and were "made to be their true selves, their child-of-God selves". Nicki's book is a gentle, authentic companion through this faith journey.
Holly Sprink, author of Faith Postures *and* Spacious

'Spiritual growth comes from taking our identity from God rather than from any other source. In this powerful book, Nicki helps us understand the security we have in God's love so we can face Him, each other and ourselves... and grow into the people we were always meant to be!'
Paul Harcourt, New Wine Regional Director (London and East) and Vicar of All Saints' Woodford Wells

Losing the fig leaf

Nicki Copeland

instant
apostle

First published in Great Britain by Instant Apostle, 2015.

Instant Apostle
The Barn
1 Watford House Lane
Watford
Herts
WD17 1BJ

British Library Cataloguing-in-Publication Data

A catalogue record for this book is available from the British Library

This book and all other Instant Apostle books are available from Instant Apostle:

Website: www.instantapostle.com

E-mail: info@instantapostle.com

ISBN 978-1-909728-32-5

Printed in Great Britain

Instant Apostle is a new way of getting ideas flowing, between followers of Jesus, and between those who would like to know more about His kingdom.

It's not just about books and it's not about a one-way information flow. It's about building a community where ideas are exchanged. Ideas will be expressed at an appropriate length. Some will take the form of books. But in many cases ideas can be expressed more briefly than in a book. Short books, or pamphlets, will be an important part of what we provide. As with pamphlets of old, these are likely to be opinionated, and produced quickly so that the community can discuss them.

Well-known authors are welcome, but we also welcome new writers. We are looking for prophetic voices, authentic and original ideas, produced at any length; quick and relevant, insightful and opinionated. And as the name implies, these will be released very quickly, either as Kindle books or printed texts or both.

Join the community. Get reading, get writing and get discussing!

Only in dependence are we strong.

Only in giving are we rich.

Only in emptying ourselves will we be filled.

Only in dying will we experience life in all its fullness.

Acknowledgements

There are many who have been a significant part of my journey – far too many to list. My thanks to all of you. I want to express particular thanks to those who have always believed in me, even when I struggled to believe in myself.

Special thanks to my husband, Pete, for your endless patience, support and encouragement. I am truly grateful to God for the gift that you are to me.

Thank you to Alex, Andrew and Emily, for all you have taught me over the years, and for the honour it is to be your mum. And thank you to my stepchildren and grandchildren, for your love and acceptance, and for the joy you bring.

Thank you to Matt, Manoj, Andy, Shaun and all who have read and commented on the manuscript. Your input has helped make the book what it is, and I am very grateful.

Above all, my thanks to God, for all You have done and are doing in my life, for entrusting me with this message and for equipping and enabling me to communicate it. This book is Yours, and my prayer is that You will use it for Your glory.

Contents

Foreword
by Shaun Lambert

For a number of years Nicki was held by the experience of feeling 'less than ordinary'. Through a heart open to God's transforming grace she was able to shift her perspective. No longer held by that experience of low self-esteem and confidence, she has been able instead to hold it, examine it lovingly and compassionately and offer it to God for transformation. In so doing she has moved from being a victim of that experience to being a witness of it. More than that, a witness who has learned skilled responses to life's ongoing challenges.

Her life has become a journey of learning to live life in all its fullness. In *Losing the fig leaf* she shares some pearls of wisdom, pearls that have been hard won – and are those worth diving for!

Nicki has blossomed from a person of prayer into a theologian – who still prays! Drawing on the latest Old and New Testament scholarship she presents a compelling vision of what it means to be made in the image of God. This is done through an examination both of the story of Adam and Eve in Genesis and of the life of Jesus as the perfect unmarred image of God who models that fully human life on offer for us.

Through her beautiful central metaphor she issues us an invitation to come out of hiding:

> Adam and Eve tried to hide from God among the trees, and they used fig leaves to hide from each other. Today we use different hiding places, and … we will explore some of these 'trees' – the six Ps – we try to hide behind, from God and each other.

The archetypal trees we hide behind that Nicki names and faces, and invites us to name and face, include those of power, possessions, productivity, perfectionism and pretence. As she unmasks them she shows us how to enter into our full inheritance as children of God.

She explains profound things clearly, and the health of the living Word of God shines through every page. As a reader you are filled with new hope for your own life.

The book calls to us to come out from our hiding places, into the light, and to let go of our fig leaves. Nicki has found her story within the Big Story of God. Read the book and find yours.

Shaun Lambert, Senior Minister, Stanmore Baptist Church; author of A Book of Sparks: A Study in Christian Mind*Full*ness

Introduction

Did you ever play hide-and-seek as a child? There's a real sense of satisfaction about finding a good hiding place, isn't there? It's quite gratifying to find a spot where you know no one will find you. There's a feeling of safety and security in the knowledge that no one can get to you.

But isn't there also an underlying fear – of exposure, of being found out? You run and hide, and all the while your heart is pumping, your mind is racing; you don't want to be caught. You know it's only a question of time before your cover is blown.

I was never particularly good at hide-and-seek. I was nearly always one of the first to be found. It is quite ironic, then, that as my life progressed, I became very good at hiding my true self and concealing who I really was.

For many years of my life I didn't like who I was and wished I could be more like someone else and less like me. Sometimes I would try to make myself someone I thought people would want to spend time with because I didn't think people would enjoy being with the person I really was. I didn't feel that I was particularly attractive to look at, or especially witty or funny, or could contribute intelligently to conversations; I didn't think I had good enough fashion sense, or artistic abilities, or that I was interesting to talk to. But then I felt that my efforts to be more 'acceptable' to people weren't good enough either, so I would end up retreating into my shell and wishing I was a fly on the wall, or that I was somewhere else entirely, because my efforts to be 'someone else' didn't work either.

Part of the problem, I think, as I look back, is that because I was so uncomfortable in my own skin, I would put my own interpretations on people's words and actions. Yet often, probably, my interpretations were wrong. If someone chose to sit somewhere else when there was an empty seat next to me, my assumption would be that the other person they chose to sit next to was, of course, far more interesting to talk to than I was. If people didn't chat to me, I naturally assumed it was because they didn't like me and because I was *soooo* boring to talk to. But if someone did choose to chat to me or to sit with me, I would be so nervous about saying something stupid or coming across as dull that I would tie myself in knots and end up fulfilling my own prophecy. Either that or I would assume that the person hadn't really wanted to talk to me or sit with me, but now that they had done, for whatever reason, I wouldn't inflict my boring personality on them! Boy, was I hard work!

Gradually, however, over a number of years, God has brought me to a place of learning to accept who I am and to enjoy being the person He has created me to be. I am learning to recognise that I do have particular strengths and certain abilities – as well as my many shortcomings – and that actually, people (for whatever strange reason) do appear to enjoy my company. Perhaps this is partly because I am more relaxed within myself now, and rather than falling over my own feet to try to impress people, I have made a decision just to be me, and if people don't like who I am, then there's not much I can do about that! Different personalities naturally gravitate towards certain people and away from others. Of course, I don't go out of my way to be obnoxious or annoying, but I have realised that there is real value in the old desktop publishing term WYSIWYG (what you see is what you get).

As I chat with people and share my story, and as people talk to me, I realise that there are many who share the same struggles as I do, and that many of us are hiding our true selves in some way or another. You can read more about my story in my first book, *Less than ordinary? My journey into finding my true self*.[1]

In this book I want to explore what being made in the image and likeness of God really means for each one of us, what it means to be 'fully human', and what it means to fully embrace our humanity and enjoy being the person we have been created to be. God made us all to be unique – there is no one else like me, or like you, on the face of the earth, nor has there ever been, and nor will there ever be.

First I want to spend a bit of time examining what it really means to be made in God's image and likeness, and considering some of the blessings God bestowed on humanity at the time of creation, and the implications of that. Then I want to look at the consequences Adam and Eve faced after they disobeyed God and ate the fruit from the tree from which God had told them not to eat, and their response to their disobedience. They tried to hide, from God and from each other. Hiding is something we still do today: we, too, try to hide from God and from each other, and I want to examine some of the ways and some of the places we try to hide – the six Ps of Power, Possessions, Productivity, Perfectionism, Pretence and Pastimes.

As we explore these hiding places, I also want to look at the way Jesus, the perfect, unmarred image of God in humanity, handled being human and to take encouragement from the way He lived His life on earth without hiding, and to suggest some practical ways we can begin to come out of our hiding places.

I believe that if we can begin to understand where we come from and who we are, this will help us work out where we are going. While we can never be truly sure where our path in life will lead us (God is always full of surprises!), if we can learn to embrace who we are and have confidence in our strengths and our abilities, as well as an awareness of our weaknesses, this gives God much greater freedom to use us in whatever way He chooses. Lack of confidence and low self-esteem inhibit us and lock us into a state of fear, leaving us unwilling to step out and take risks. So we choose to stay among the trees where we know it's safe and where the risk of failure is smaller. It's so much easier to stay hidden away than to step out, to face exposure and to feel vulnerable.

Sometimes we invite God in to our hiding places with us, instead of stepping out from them with Him. We know He loves us and wants a relationship with us, and we want a relationship with Him – but we want it to be on our terms. God is gracious, and I believe He does join us in those cramped, dark places – He loves us so much He just wants to be with us. But He also longs for us to take the hand He is offering and to step out with Him. We might feel safe and comfortable where we are, especially if God is there with us, but there is so much more to be enjoyed beyond the trees, if only we would have the courage to walk out with Him. He is offering us the opportunity to sing and to dance with Him, to express who we really are, to enjoy true freedom.

Over the last few years I have taken a few risks, stepped out from some of my own hiding places and done some things I never dreamed I would do. I'm still not sure where the road is heading, but one thing I can tell you is that the journey is exciting, and I'm really enjoying the ride! Yes, it's taking me way out of my comfort zone at times, and some things have been really hard to do, but my heavenly Father has been with me all the way, holding my hand and leading me forward, step by step. I know there is so much more to come, and I'm looking forward to discovering what else He has in store for me.

I also know that at times it will be difficult, and that I'm going to have to face more of my fears and insecurities along the way. But I know that God will help me do that too, as and when these times come.

I hope this book will encourage you to take the hand that God is offering you, to allow Him to lead you out of some of your hiding places and to walk with Him on the path He has set out for you. God has a Big Plan for your life – an important role in

His Big Story – and I want to encourage you to embrace what He has planned for you.

A final thought: it's not easy to go about the practical business of daily living – working, eating, caring for ourselves and our families, and so on – if we're holding something in our hand. Imagine trying to prepare dinner with one hand because you're holding a big leaf in the other to hide behind, or driving to work with a tree branch in your hand. Holding on to our fig leaves restricts us, inhibits us and reduces our freedom to move and live. They get in the way and are a real nuisance! We need both hands to live as we were truly created to live!

Let me encourage you to step out from among the trees, to let go of your fig leaves and to enjoy the freedom of living without them! Live your life in the way God intended you to live it!

Notes

[1] Nicki Copeland, *Less than ordinary? My journey into finding my true self* (Watford: Instant Apostle, 2013).

Chapter 1
The image of God

Then God said, 'Let us make humankind in our
image, according to our likeness; and let them have
dominion over the fish of the sea, and over the
birds of the air, and over the cattle, and over all the
wild animals of the earth, and over every creeping
thing that creeps upon the earth.'
So God created humankind in his image,
in the image of God he created them;
male and female he created them.
Genesis 1:26-27

Have you ever thought about what it really means to be made in
the image of God? As I have been exploring this, I have
discovered that it means a whole lot more than I ever realised!
My interpretation had always been simply that it meant we were
created to be distinct from the animals and were endowed with
certain 'spiritual' qualities that set us apart from the rest of
creation. This is true, but there is a whole lot more besides!

Before we can consider some of the places where we hide and
the reasons why, it is important that we understand who we
really are and what we were created for. As I mentioned in the
introduction, we need to work out where we have come from in
order to begin to understand where we are going. Unless we
know who we were created to be, we cannot fully embrace what
God has created us to be and to do. God created us in His image
and after His likeness, and while this of course implies some
common characteristics for all of us, it has some very specific

implications for each one of us individually. God has created us all to be different, and His image looks a little different in each of us. He has planted different aspects of His character in every person so that all of humanity collectively can express who He is to one another and to His creation.

As far as I am concerned, God created me to be a woman of about five foot seven, of average build, with brown hair and green eyes. He created me to have particular qualities that might be deemed to be 'feminine', such as my taste in clothes and my liking for the colours pink and purple. He gave me a love for words, and I have a particular fondness for sweet things – especially anything chocolatey! He gave me the ability to organise and be organised, despite the fact that I'm not always very tidy! And I am discovering new things about myself all the time as God continues to work in me and to grow His image and likeness within me.

Evolution, the Big Bang, or God?

There are two creation accounts in Genesis – the first in Genesis 1:1–2:4 and the second in 2:4-25. There are some subtle differences between the two accounts – or perhaps, different emphases. The first account is written in the form of poetry, and the second more as a narrative account. Do we take them literally – that God really made the earth and everything in it in six days and then rested? How long was a 'day' – a segment of 24 hours of time as we know it, or could each 'day' have been a much longer period of time – even a thousand years – as might be suggested if we consider what 2 Peter 3:8 tells us, that 'with the Lord one day is like a thousand years, and a thousand years are like one day'? Can we equate the Genesis accounts with the theory of evolution or the Big Bang theory, or do we have to discount these altogether?

I'm not going to attempt to answer these questions here. Whatever we believe about the creation accounts, and whether we view them as literal or figurative, the key is to remember that Genesis was written to tell the people of God something about God, and to tell them something about themselves. Rather than simply focusing on the events, we need to explore what these accounts are telling us about God, about ourselves, and about our relationship with Him – both the relationship of the whole of humanity with God through history, and our own individual, personal relationship with Him.

So what do these creation accounts tell us, then, about what it means to be made in God's image? None of the animals is described as being made in God's image – only human beings. What makes us different? Well, they tell us that we are made in the image of God physically as well as that we have a spiritual likeness. (Some biblical scholars call these 'natural' and 'supernatural' qualities.) In addition, and just as importantly, we were created with a relational likeness to God.

Let's explore each of these in turn.

Physical likeness

It might seem strange to suggest that we are made to resemble God physically, as God is spirit and does not have a physical body. God is infinite and has no limitations, and by saying that we resemble Him physically, I in no way want to suggest that God is defined by the limits of human physiology. However, if we look at the Bible text, it does appear to suggest that we are made in God's physical image.

The Hebrew uses two words to describe our resemblance to God, as we can see from Genesis 1:26 (above): 'Let us make humankind in our *image* [*tselem*], according to our *likeness* [*demuth*]' (my emphasis).

The word *tselem* is defined as 'a representative *figure*, especially an *idol*'.[1] Elsewhere in the Old Testament the word is used to refer to an external, physical image, very often a statue or an idol. For example, in Numbers 33:52 God says to Moses, 'you shall ... destroy all their cast images [*tselem*]', and in Ezekiel 16:17 God says to the people, 'You also took your beautiful jewels of my gold and my silver that I had given you, and made for yourself male images [*tselem*].' Clearly these are created copies, made to physically look like the originals.

So how we can bear a physical resemblance to God if He doesn't have a physical body? God is infinite, limitless, eternal and unbounded, and as I said earlier, we must be careful not to try to 'shrink' Him to the limits of humanity. But the imagery perhaps helps us to relate and to understand. I believe that if God *were* to have a physical form, He would look like a human being. Biblical commentator David Atkinson explains it this way: 'If God were to come among us within the constraints of this physical world, he would be a human being.'[2] Indeed, when God did come among us, He came as a human being, in the form of the man Jesus Christ. As Colossians 1:15 tells us, 'He is the image of the invisible God'.

There are hints in the Old Testament of God actually making use of a physical form. God walks in the Garden of Eden in the cool of the day in Genesis 3:8. Jacob wrestles with God and says, 'I have seen God face to face, and yet my life is preserved' (Genesis 32:30). Exodus 33:11 tells us that God would 'speak to Moses face to face, as one speaks to a friend'. And in verses 20 to 23 of the same chapter, God says to Moses:

> 'You cannot see my face; for no one shall see me and live.' And the Lord continued, 'See, there is a place by me where you shall stand on the rock; and while my glory passes by I will put you in a cleft of the rock, and I will cover you with my hand until I have passed by;

then I will take away my hand, and you shall see my
back; but my face shall not be seen.'

And in Isaiah 6:1, Isaiah 'saw the Lord sitting on a throne,
high and lofty; and the hem of his robe filled the temple'.

So God created human beings to resemble the way He would
look if He were to have a physical body. God created you – and
me – to resemble Him. And He created every other human being
to resemble Him too.

How much do we value this physical image of God in
ourselves, in other people? Do we value the incredible variety
that He has created, or do we have a fixed idea of what the
'perfect' human being should look like?

Do we judge and value people by the way they look, or do we
look deeper at who they are inside? How do we respond and
react to people whose physical form doesn't 'fit' our concept of
the perfect body?

How do we feel about our own bodies? Do I embrace the
image of God in the way I look, or am I dissatisfied with my
appearance? How much do I bow to pressure to conform to what
the world views as acceptable?

We'll come back to this later, when we look at the tree of
Perfectionism. Suffice it to say for now that there is tremendous
pressure to measure up to the world's idea of beauty rather than
measuring our worth by God's standards. We fear what other
people think of us and we try to hide, for fear of being found
wanting.

Spiritual likeness

The word *demuth* ('likeness') is also used in the Bible to denote
resemblance, and it tends to be used to convey similarity rather
than an identical copy – perhaps a 'spiritual' or an abstract
likeness.[3] It comes from the Hebrew root *damah*, which means 'to

resemble, to be like'.[4] Scholars suggest that it is used to modify the term *tselem* in order to prevent an overly physical understanding of the image of God in humanity.[5]

Other instances of *demuth/damah* in Scripture that convey likeness or similarity include Isaiah 40:18, which says, 'To whom then will you liken [*damah*] God, or what likeness [*demuth*] compare with him?' Psalm 58:4 describes the wickedness of the people, saying, 'They have venom like [*demuth*] the venom of a serpent.'

Some of these spiritual, or supernatural, qualities have been described as those characteristics that set humanity apart from the animals. Theologian Wayne Grudem identified five traits that distinguish human beings from the rest of creation: moral, spiritual, mental, relational and physical.[6] St Augustine suggested that the image of God is visible in the way human beings are able to express emotions – particularly love.[7] Perhaps we could add that human beings have greater degrees of self-awareness, the ability to think rationally, intelligence, highly evolved communication skills, memory and the ability to make moral and considered decisions rather than acting purely on instinct.

A helpful way of understanding the physical and spiritual similarity is to consider the way children resemble their parents. Genesis 5:3 uses these same terms, *demuth* and *tselem*, when it tells us that Adam had a son 'in his own likeness, according to his image'. Children are born with a physical likeness to their parents and, to a greater or lesser extent, with similar characteristics and personality traits. As they grow and spend more time with their parents, they learn the habits, mannerisms and ways of their parents, and so become more like them.

Many times I have heard myself repeating things to my own children that my mum used to say to me when I was growing up. Things like, 'Take your coat off indoors, or you won't feel the benefit when you go outside,' and 'I worry about you because I love you.' And I hear my children repeating things they hear me saying too. I had to stifle my laughter when my daughter, when she was much younger, told her granddad to go and sit on the naughty step and think about his behaviour! Fortunately he saw the funny side.

In the same way, we are born with certain similarities to our heavenly Father – physical and spiritual – and as we spend time with Him, we become more like Him as we learn and adopt His ways and habits. Children learn what pleases their parents, and (we hope!) will choose to do things that please their parents as they grow up and grow older. We, too, as we grow, learn what pleases our heavenly Father, and we also endeavour to do what pleases Him. Paul in 2 Corinthians 3:18 reminds us that we are all 'being transformed into the same image from one degree of glory to another; for this comes from the Lord, the Spirit'.

I long to see more of God's likeness in me. I remember a song by Amy Grant that I used to enjoy in the 1980s which talked about her desire to have her Father's eyes.[8] She sings about how she would want to be remembered as having eyes that are just like her Father's, eyes that are compassionate, understanding and helpful. She wants to be known as someone who is just like her Father. I loved that song because it expressed a desire that I had too, and still have, to be just like my heavenly Father. Yet I struggled with wanting to be like other people too, to feel that I fitted in, to feel accepted.

So often we are caught in a dilemma of wanting to be transformed by God, yet we are also pulled by the things of this world. As we look later at the six Ps, the trees behind which we hide, we will also look at Jesus, the perfect human being who revealed what the true image of God in humanity looks like, and how He truly resembled His Father without bowing to pressure to conform to what the world wanted Him to be.

Relational likeness

As well as the physical and spiritual resemblance, there is a third way in which humans are created to resemble God: relational likeness. God, as we know, exists in a threefold relationship in the form of the Trinity – Father, Son and Holy Spirit. He is three Persons in one God. It is interesting to note that the very first words God speaks in the Bible are, 'Let us …' (Genesis 1:26). Who is 'us'? Some suggest that here God is speaking to the courts of heavenly beings, but perhaps He is talking to Himself – as God the Father to the other Persons of the Trinitarian Godhead.

Human beings are created to live in relationships too, with God, with each other and with the rest of creation. I'm sure we've all heard the saying, 'No man is an island' – a phrase that was first used as long ago as the seventeenth century.[9] This is so true. No one can live completely independently of other people. We need other people around us to satisfy our physical and practical needs, our emotional needs and our intellectual needs.

To need other people is not a weakness. Independence is a good thing, and indeed it is necessary, but it all has to be kept in balance. Too much independence and we are in danger of becoming that island, of cutting off everyone around us and living in isolation. This is not healthy, either for us or for anyone else. If we deprive ourselves of other people and their input into our lives, we will not only miss out on much joy, but we will also miss out on vital keys to our development as human beings. And they will be missing out on the benefits of a relationship with us, too!

I'm sure we have all known people who think they can do it on their own, who believe they don't need the input of other people. I have known Christians who think they can live out the fullness of God's plan for their lives without living in Christian community. Personally, I don't believe this is possible – this is not what God wants for us (other than those, of course, who are called to live such a lifestyle, but that is rare). Time and again I have seen such people struggle and lose their way. We all need the support, the love and the accountability of living in community with others. God knows what He is doing!

John Bowlby was a British psychologist, psychiatrist and psychoanalyst who carried out research into child development and attachment theory. His research into the impact of the separation of children from their parents during the Second World War has had a huge bearing on the way orphans are cared for today. Subsequently, research was carried out among children brought up in an orphanage compared to children brought up by foster families, and it was discovered that those looked after in the institution were slower to develop in terms of play, speech and social skills than those cared for in a family environment with foster parents. The orphanage was clean and in good condition, and the children received nutritious meals and appropriate medical care – so all their practical needs were met. The only difference was the amount of attention and touch they received from adults.[10]

Jesus, the perfect, unmarred image of God in the world, showed us how to live in relationships. He had a very close relationship with God His Father and regularly took time out to pray and spend time with Him. Jesus also had an intimate group of close friends, a wider circle of disciples and followers, and many acquaintances. These relationships were the ideal way not only to set an example to His friends and followers of the right way to live, but also to model to us the importance of living in relationship with others. Jesus lived what He preached, and by spending so much time with Him in such close proximity, His disciples could learn from His example. What better way is there to teach than to be a good role model?

This isn't to say, of course, that all of Jesus' relationships were harmonious – we know they weren't. It goes without saying that

Jesus loved every person He came across, but there was conflict. His first priority was to God the Father and to be obedient to Him, and where this did not match up with what other people wanted Him to do, He would always do what God wanted Him to do, no matter what the consequences might be.

Male and female

The importance of relationships is demonstrated further by the fact that God created both male and female, saying, 'It is not good that the man should be alone; I will make him a helper as his partner' (Genesis 2:18). Theologian Andrew Perriman points out that 'helper' here is not intended to imply the idea of subordination or servanthood. The Hebrew for 'helper' is *ezer*, and describes someone who rushes to help another who is in difficulty. Perriman says that the helper 'is an independent person who makes up a significant deficiency or helplessness in the other'[11] and points out that this word in the Old Testament is often used to refer to God, who is Israel's 'helper' in times of trouble – for example:

> But I am poor and needy;
> hasten to me, O God!
> You are my help [*ezer*] and my deliverer;
> O Lord, do not delay!
> *Psalm 70:5*

It is interesting that the NRSVA version of the Bible translates Genesis 2:18 as 'a helper as his partner'. Other translations offer slightly different interpretations, such as 'a helper suitable for him' (NIV UK) or 'a helper comparable to him' (NKJV). It could also be translated as 'corresponding to', which perhaps suggests even more clearly the equality of the woman to the man.

The relationship between the man and the woman was originally intended to be complementary, to be equal, each using their own particular strengths for the common good. The idea of man 'ruling over' woman is a result of the Fall. The imbalance of power in relationships is something that human beings have struggled with ever since, and power is one of the biggest trees behind which we hide. We will come back to these thoughts in later chapters.

So good!

One final thought before we move on. All through Genesis 1, when God looks at what He has created, the Bible says that He saw that it was good (verses 4, 10, 12, 18, 21 and 25). But in verse 31, we are told, 'God saw everything that he had made, and indeed, it was very good.' This was after He had created humankind. Everything God had created before was good, but once He had created human beings – male and female – it was *very* good. This suggests that God was very pleased with His creation of human beings, and that they enhanced the rest of His creation – they were the icing on the cake, so to speak – and it was now complete.

It is interesting to note that in the second creation account, before God created the woman, He observed that 'It is *not* good that the man should be alone' (Genesis 2:18, my emphasis). This provides a striking contrast to the repetition in the previous chapter of all that God had created which was good. God clearly recognised the need of human beings to live in community, in relationships. Solitude is not good, according to God, and He worked immediately to address the problem

So you and I have been created in the image and after the likeness of God – physically, spiritually and relationally. But what relevance does that have for us here and now in the twenty-first century? Well, God had a plan for creation, and a plan for humanity. After He created the humans, God blessed them and gave them a job to do…

Notes

[1] 'to *shade*; a *phantom*, that is, (figuratively) *illusion, resemblance*; hence a representative *figure*, especially an *idol*'. Dictionaries of Hebrew and Greek From *Strong's exhaustive concordance* by James Strong (1890), via e-Sword Bible software.

[2] David Atkinson, *The message of Genesis 1-11* (Leicester, Inter-Varsity Press, 1990), p.36.

[3] R. Larry Overstreet, 'Man in the image of God: A reappraisal', *Criswell Theological Review* (2005) 43-70, p.65.

[4] Strong defines it as '*resemblance*; concretely *model, shape*; adverbially *like:* – fashion, like (-ness, as), manner, similitude.' *Strong's exhaustive concordance* (via e-Sword Bible software*).

[5] J. Richard Middleton, *The liberating image: The Imago Dei in Genesis 1* (Grand Rapids, MI: Brazos Press, 2005), p.25.

[6] Cited in Overstreet, 'Man in the image of God', p.53.

[7] W. Sibley Towner, 'Clones of God: Genesis 1:26-28 and the image of God in the Hebrew Bible', *Interpretation*, (2005), p.343.

[8] Gary Winthur Chapman, 'Father's eyes', from the album *My Father's eyes* (1979).

[9] John Donne (1572–1631), from 'Devotions upon emergent occasions and several steps in my sickness – Meditation XVII' (1624).

[10] Craig Greenfield, 'Touch-starved: The hunger of children in orphanages', from *The urban halo: A story of hope for orphans of the poor*. Available at http://unitingforchildren.org/2013/05/touch-starved/ (accessed 24th June 2014).

[11] Andrew Perriman, 'A helper fit for him', 31st January 2012, from P.OST: An Evangelical Theology for the age to come. Available at http://www.postost.net/2012/01/helper-fit-him (accessed 10th August 2014).

Chapter 2
Blessed – to be a blessing

God blessed them, and God said to them, 'Be
fruitful and multiply, and fill the earth and subdue
it; and have dominion over the fish of the sea and
over the birds of the air and over every living thing
that moves upon the earth.'

Genesis 1:28

God 'blessed' the humans He had created. But what exactly does this mean? What was the blessing? The way we often understand 'blessing' is to mean a few generalised words that convey a desire for good things to be bestowed on the one receiving the blessing. 'May God bless you' – usually translates in our minds as, 'May God give you good things so that you can enjoy a happy, peaceful and trouble-free life.'

Was this the kind of blessing God gave to Adam and Eve? Was it a general, vague, 'Don't worry – I'll be with you and you'll have a great life' kind of blessing? No. God's words that instruct the humans to be fruitful, to multiply, to fill the earth, to subdue it, to have dominion over all the living things – these words *are* the blessing!

I have to confess, it took me a little while to get my head around this. I had always understood this verse as God doing two separate things: giving the man and the woman a general blessing and *then* the instruction He gave them to be fruitful and fill the earth. But as we look at some of the other blessings God gave, we can see a pattern beginning to form – of blessing and commissioning going hand in hand. The first is His blessing to Noah and his family after they left the ark following the flood:

> God blessed Noah and his sons, and said to them, 'Be
> fruitful and multiply, and fill the earth.'
> *Genesis 9:1*

Have you ever noticed how the words of this blessing are
exactly the same as the blessing given to Adam and Eve in
Genesis 1:28 – to 'be fruitful and multiply, and fill the earth'?

Let's look at another of God's blessings – to Abraham in
Genesis 12:2-3:

> 'I will make of you a great nation, and I will bless you,
> and make your name great, so that you will be a
> blessing. I will bless those who bless you, and the one
> who curses you I will curse; and in you all the families
> of the earth shall be blessed.'

The key words here are, 'so that you will be a blessing'. God
will bless Abraham *in order that* he will be a blessing to others.
He will bless Abraham's offspring *in order that* through them 'all
the families of the earth' will be blessed. Abraham receives God's
blessing in order that other people will be blessed.

Abraham is again blessed by God in Genesis 22, and the
nations of the earth shall be blessed as a result of his obedience
to God:

> 'I will indeed bless you, and I will make your offspring
> as numerous as the stars of heaven and as the sand that
> is on the seashore. And your offspring shall possess the
> gate of their enemies, and by your offspring shall all the
> nations of the earth gain blessing for themselves,
> because you have obeyed my voice.'
> *Genesis 22:17-18*

In Genesis 26, God reminds Isaac of His promises to his father
Abraham:

Reside in this land as an alien, and I will be with you, and will bless you; for to you and to your descendants I will give all these lands, and I will fulfil the oath that I swore to your father Abraham. I will make your offspring as numerous as the stars of heaven, and will give to your offspring all these lands; and all the nations of the earth shall gain blessing for themselves through your offspring, because Abraham obeyed my voice and kept my charge, my commandments, my statutes, and my laws.'
Genesis 26:3-5

In Genesis 28 Jacob has a dream in which God stands beside him and says:

'I am the Lord, the God of Abraham your father and the God of Isaac; the land on which you lie I will give to you and to your offspring; and your offspring shall be like the dust of the earth, and you shall spread abroad to the west and to the east and to the north and to the south; and all the families of the earth shall be blessed in you and in your offspring. Know that I am with you and will keep you wherever you go, and will bring you back to this land; for I will not leave you until I have done what I have promised you.'
Genesis 28:13-15

So God blesses His people *in order that* they will be a blessing to others. The blessing is to be shared, to be passed on. When God blesses His people, He fills them up to overflowing, so that the blessing will spill over to bless others in turn. Perhaps this is obvious, but all too often we miss the point. I know I do – so often in my life I have wanted God's blessings for myself, simply because I want to be blessed, I want a happy life and good things for myself and my family. I haven't necessarily thought about what God might want me to do with His blessings once I receive them. But while God loves to bless His people – and He does shower blessings upon us just because He loves to give us good things – it doesn't always work that way. God's blessings are given for the benefit of everyone, and He wants us to share the good things He gives.

Often, when God blesses His people, the blessing comes hand in hand with a task in order to ensure that the blessing is shared. Adam and Eve were to multiply and fill the earth *in order* to be a blessing to the earth. Noah and his family were blessed *in order* to be fruitful and multiply and fill the earth, in the same way Adam and Eve had been blessed and instructed to fill the earth. Abraham, Isaac and Jacob were blessed *in order* that they and their descendants would be a blessing to all the families of the earth.

At first glance, this might appear that God's blessing is conditional – that we will only be blessed if we do what God says. I guess in some ways that's true, because the task *is* the blessing, so we cannot receive the blessing if we do not carry out the instruction. But because the task is a blessing, there is real joy in doing it anyway! A blessing by its very nature is a good thing, so it stands to reason that to carry out the instructions God gives in a blessing would be a blessing in itself to the person carrying it out, doesn't it?

Sharing our blessings is a natural response to and outworking of God's love and goodness to us. As James points out, 'faith without works is … dead' (James 2:26).

Let's look in a little more detail at what God's blessing in Genesis 1:28 actually means.

'Be fruitful and multiply'

In Genesis 1:20-21, God created all the creatures of the sea and all the birds of the air, and then in verse 22:

God blessed them, saying, 'Be fruitful and multiply and
fill the waters in the seas, and let birds multiply on the
earth.'

In verses 24 and 25 God made the living creatures of the earth
and, although the Bible doesn't say this, I think we can assume
that the same blessing would have been given to them.

Along with these other creatures, then, human beings are told
to multiply and fill the earth. The first thing we notice here is that
fruitfulness – procreation – is a blessing from God. God created
humankind to be male and female. This was a deliberate
decision on God's part, and He chose that humanity would
procreate via the union of male and female. He could quite easily
have chosen for procreation to happen some other way, but this
was the decision He made. Nothing that God does is accidental,
and I believe this means that the union of male and female within
the sacred marriage relationship is a part of God's blessing, a gift
to humanity. We have already established that humankind's
ability to express love is a part of the image of God within us, as
is the fact that we are beings created for relationships.

It is also important to notice here that when God made human
beings to be male and female, the blessing and the task were
given to them both. The Hebrew for the word translated by the
NRSVA as 'humankind' in Genesis 1:26 ('Let us make
humankind in our image, according to our likeness') is *adamah*,
translated in some versions of the Bible as 'man'. But *adamah* is a
generic word for 'humankind'; it does not mean just the male of
the species. The words for 'male' and 'female' in verse 27 are two
different words – *zakar* and *neqebah* respectively. And in verse 26
God says, 'And let *them* have dominion' (my emphasis). God
created humankind, and out of it, in His wisdom, He brought
male and female.

'Have dominion'

The instruction to 'subdue [the earth] and have dominion' is pretty clear: human beings were given authority over the rest of creation, to manage it and to rule it.

The English word 'dominion' today is often understood to mean ruling in a forceful and overbearing way. Indeed, the first definition of 'dominion' in the Oxford English Dictionary is, 'The power or right of governing and controlling'.[1] The words 'power', 'right' and 'controlling' might suggest that the rest of creation is there purely for the benefit of humankind, to do as we please with. But this is not what God had in mind.

The word 'subdue' comes from the Hebrew *kabash*, and the term 'have dominion' is from *radah*. These are often linked in the Old Testament to kingship, which would strongly suggest that human beings have a royal calling to be God's representatives on the earth. And as God's representatives, we are called to rule the earth in the way that God would rule it, and our relationship with the earth should reflect the relationship that God has with us. This is not a harsh, tyrannical rule, but a gentle, tender reign that is characterised by love.

We need to remember that the earth belongs to its Creator, and that we are to look after it, in the same way a gardener might be employed to look after a domestic garden or an area of parkland. The gardener will tend it and take care of it, but it still belongs to the owner/employer. The owner trusts the gardener to follow his instructions and to manage the garden in the way he wants it to be managed. If the gardener were to mistreat the garden or disobey the given instructions, he would more than likely lose his job, or at the very least face consequences for his actions.

Adam and Eve were told that they were to take care of the garden on God's behalf. They were given clear instructions, and the restrictions were very few. In fact, there was only one restriction – there was just one tree from which God did not want the humans to eat. Otherwise, they were free to do whatever they chose, to live within and to live out the blessing He had bestowed upon them.

Blessings for you and me!

So God's blessings are given for the benefit of everyone – to be shared with the whole of creation – not just for the individual recipients of the particular blessing. The earth was entrusted to human beings to look after it and to manage it in a loving, mutually beneficial relationship, and to fill it with lots more human beings who would also enjoy a relationship with their loving Creator.

God has a plan for each of our lives – for your life and for mine. And to fully engage with this plan we need to receive it as a blessing, as a gift from Him. Yet it isn't easy to receive a gift from someone if we are trying to hide from them, or if we are already holding something in our hands. If we are hiding among the trees, or holding on to our fig leaves, then we can only partially receive the blessing God wants to pour upon us and into our lives.

Noah could have chosen not to build the ark. Abraham could have chosen to stay where he was rather than to leave his home and travel to the new place where God was leading him. But they didn't: they chose to trust God and did – let's face it – some pretty strange things. Would I have had the courage to build a huge boat miles away from any body of water? Would I have had the faith to leave my home and travel somewhere new, not even knowing where I was going? Yet because of their obedience, and the obedience of many people through the ages, God was able to fulfil His plans.

What does God want me to do so that I can be fully immersed in His blessings and His plans for my life? If I stay in my hiding place, what will I be missing out on? What might others be missing out on?

Notes

[1] Oxford English Dictionary online. Available at
http://www.oed.com/view/Entry/56717?rskey=qSWsWT&result=1
(accessed 24th June 2014. Subscription may be necessary).

Chapter 3
And then it all went wrong...

So when the woman saw that the tree was good
for food, and that it was a delight to the eyes, and
that the tree was to be desired to make one wise,
she took of its fruit and ate; and she also gave
some to her husband, who was with her, and he ate.

Genesis 3:6

Sadly, as we know, it all became very messy in the garden. Along came the serpent and tempted the humans, offering them knowledge and wisdom. The serpent suggested that they should eat of the tree from which they had been told not to eat – the tree of the knowledge of good and evil – and said to them, 'When you eat of it your eyes will be opened, and you will be like God, knowing good and evil' (Genesis 3:5). This was very appealing – the thought of gaining knowledge and the prospect of being 'like God' were very tempting. The sad irony was that Adam and Eve already *were* like God because they had been made in His image and according to His likeness.

In God's original brief to the man in Genesis 2 when He placed him in the garden, God gave him instructions to work it and take care of it. If, however, the man were to eat from the tree of the knowledge of good and evil, he would die:

'You may freely eat of every tree of the garden; but of
the tree of the knowledge of good and evil you shall not
eat, for in the day that you eat of it you shall die.'
Genesis 2:16-17

The man and woman could eat from every other tree in the garden, which means that, at that time, they were permitted to eat from the tree of life.

The reason God had told the humans not to eat of the tree of the knowledge of good and evil was for their protection. He wasn't a killjoy who wanted to spoil their fun by keeping the best fruit from them. Neither did He want to play a game with them and test them to see how long they could resist the temptation. God knew what they could handle, and He knew that they would not be able to cope with the knowledge of good and evil, so He forbade them to eat of the fruit.

But Adam and Eve thought they knew better than God. They listened to the lies of the serpent, disobeyed God's instruction and ate from the tree. When they ate of its fruit, 'the eyes of both were opened, and they knew that they were naked' (Genesis 3:7). The word 'knew' here has been defined as 'properly to ascertain by *seeing*',[1] so their eyes had indeed been opened. They saw; they knew; they understood.

Hiding from each other

The first thing the man and the woman did was to sew fig leaves together to make clothes for themselves to cover their nakedness (verse 7). Why was their nakedness suddenly an issue? They had always been naked – since the day they had been created. Why, now that their eyes had been opened, did it bother them so much that the first thing they felt compelled to do was to cover themselves up? I suggest that it was because they felt exposed and vulnerable. They were now able to discern good and evil, since they had eaten from the tree, and they were filled with shame because of what they had done, because of their disobedience.

I'm sure we are all familiar with that feeling: if we do something wrong, our shame makes us want to hide ourselves away from others. I know it all too well, unfortunately. I am all too familiar with that sick, heavy feeling in the pit of my stomach when I know I have said something to someone that I shouldn't have said, or done something I shouldn't have done. I recognise how I would much prefer to hide away and not have to face them any time soon. I am acutely aware of my embarrassment the next time I see them and know I need to apologise.

Adam and Eve were no different – they were ashamed, and they wanted to hide from each other.

Hiding from God

The second thing the man and the woman did was to try to hide from God. Genesis 3:8 tells us:

> They heard the sound of the Lord God walking in the garden at the time of the evening breeze, and the man and his wife hid themselves from the presence of the Lord God among the trees of the garden.

They were ashamed of what they had done. God, of course, had been right all along – they could not cope with their new knowledge. It's interesting that when God asked them where they were, the man responded by saying that he was hiding out of fear *because he was naked*, and not because of what he had done. Already there is distortion of the facts and deliberate, careful selection in his reply because he doesn't want to own up to what he has done. God's response – 'Who told you that you were naked?' (verse 11) – confirms that not only had their nakedness not been an issue for them before they ate from the tree, but also that they hadn't even been aware of their nakedness.

By giving in to temptation and disobeying God, Adam and Eve shifted their focus away from God and on to themselves. Instead of focusing on God, on His blessing and on the job He had given them to do, what they wanted became their priority instead – to have knowledge and to 'be like God'. They had already been given so much, but rather than focusing on everything they had been given, they wanted the one thing they hadn't been given – the fruit from the one forbidden tree. How often are we guilty of doing the same? I know myself how easy it is to want what I do not have, instead of focusing on the many, many blessings God has given to me, and being grateful for them.

Consequences

There were consequences for Adam and Eve of their disobedience. Its effects on the physical, spiritual and relational image and likeness of God in humanity were catastrophic.

Physical consequences

In terms of the physical image, the consequences, as God had warned, were death. Adam and Eve should by rights have been wiped out. But instead of allowing them to reap this consequence of their action, God chose to spare them and began to put together a Rescue Plan which would mean the death of another in their place, and in the place of all of fallen humanity. God sent Jesus, the second Adam, or 'last Adam' (1 Corinthians 15:45), so that humanity could be spared and eventually restored. However, in the meantime, the physical image of God in humanity was severely distorted. Death had indeed made its entry into the world, and physical decay, ageing, sickness and pain now became a part of humankind's daily reality.

The physical image of God in humanity was now severely deformed, and the physical body would die. God said to Adam:

'By the sweat of your face
you shall eat bread

until you return to the ground,
for out of it you were taken;
you are dust,
and to dust you shall return.'
Genesis 3:19

Adam and Eve had to leave the Garden of Eden, and the idyllic lifestyle that was all they had known. Strangely enough, this was for their own protection. Previously, they had been free to eat from the tree of life, as eternal life was already theirs. However, now that sin had entered the world, creation had been spoiled, and death and decay had become part of humankind's reality, God did not want them to live for ever in the mess that had been made. God could not now allow Adam and Eve to eat from the tree of life – He loved them too much to let them live in that mess for ever – so they had to leave the beautiful garden.

Spiritual consequences

The spiritual resemblance of humanity to God had also been badly damaged. God is, of course, sinless, and now humankind had been tainted by sin. I'm sure I don't need to go into details of how the character of men and women has moved far away from its original created likeness to God. Self-giving love has given way to selfishness, and our decision-making ability is severely damaged so that the decisions we make are not always wise and sensible, to say the least. Our motivations are impure, and our focus is on ourselves and our own wants, often at the expense of others' needs. As Adam and Eve lost their focus on God, the attention of the whole of humanity became pointed at 'self', and our instincts now are self-serving and narrow.

The voice of God has become distorted to our ears, and because we have become so accustomed to listening to the lies of the enemy, the enemy's voice is often louder in our ears than the voice of God. The voice of the enemy might take any number of forms, and it is often very difficult to recognise. It might be our own wants and desires pushing us to act in a particular way, or others tempting us to do something we know we shouldn't. It could be the culture we live in and the worldview we hold, and the worldview that those around us hold. It might be prejudices and attitudes that we have grown up with. It might be physical temptations, such as addictions to alcohol or drugs or other substances, or the drive to satisfy sexual urges inappropriately. It might be the compulsion for material wealth and possessions. The list goes on...

Relational consequences
Humanity's relationships were now permanently damaged too.

With God: The relationship of the man and the woman with God could not now be the same as it was before. The close relationship they had previously enjoyed was changed, and now that the man and woman had sinned and disobeyed God, a barrier had been erected between them, a barrier that could only be removed through the fulfilment of God's Rescue Plan. Yet God did not turn His back on them.

We saw earlier how the man and the woman hid from God when He walked in the garden. God already knew what they had done, yet He still chose to walk with them; He still wanted to be with them and to be in companionship with them. But they distanced themselves from Him, and humankind has been running away and trying to hide from God ever since.

With each other: The relationship of the man and woman with each other was no longer the idyllic, equal relationship it had been before. This can be seen right away, in the way they reply to God's question, 'Have you eaten of the tree of which I commanded you not to eat?' (Genesis 3:11). The man's response was straight away to blame the woman, and the woman's response was to immediately blame the serpent. They could not accept responsibility for what they had done – perhaps it was too big, and their shame was too great. They could not cope with the guilt, and they knew they couldn't make things right again, so the easiest thing was to find someone else to blame. Sounds familiar, doesn't it?

The balance of the relationship between men and women was now distorted. God said to the woman:

> 'I will greatly increase your pangs in childbearing;
> in pain you shall bring forth children,
> yet your desire shall be for your husband,
> and he shall rule over you.'
> *Genesis 3:16*

Sandra Richter suggests this means that the previous equality of relationship between the man and the woman will from now on be characterised by competition and striving. The instincts of the woman will still be for mothering and nurturing, but the fulfilment of these will be subject to a power struggle within the relationship with the man.[2] Andrew Perriman agrees:

> Nothing is said prior to the expulsion from the garden
> about the subordination of the woman to the man …
> The rule of the man over the woman is a consequence
> of the fall, part of the curse against the woman, not an
> aspect of the original created relationship.[3]

As well as this, childbirth became painful. I wonder what giving birth would have been like before… As a mother of three, I can testify that it certainly is a physically painful experience! Yet it is also something incredibly beautiful, and out of the pain comes tremendous joy and blessing.

With the earth: The previously harmonious relationship of humanity with the earth would also now be characterised by a struggle for power. Stewarding the earth from now on would be hard and often fruitless work. The ground would no longer naturally respond to humanity's authority, and there would be no guarantee that the man and the woman would even be able to obtain what they would need for their daily food and other needs:

> 'Cursed is the ground because of you;
> in toil you shall eat of it all the days of your life;
> thorns and thistles it shall bring forth for you;
> and you shall eat the plants of the field.
> By the sweat of your face
> you shall eat bread
> until you return to the ground,
> for out of it you were taken;
> you are dust
> and to dust you shall return.'
> *Genesis 3:17-19*

Still today, farmers and crop growers are dependent on the right weather for an ample harvest. There are numerous threats to their income and livelihood. If there is insufficient rain, the crops won't grow enough. If there is too much rain at the wrong time, they will be washed out. Battles with weeds, the 'thorns and thistles it shall bring forth', are ongoing, as is the necessity to try to prevent crops being eaten by birds and animals.

I confess great admiration for anyone who is able to grow plants. My fingers are definitely not green. I love having plants in the house, but sadly they never last long. I don't know why: I water them – not too much, not too little; I give them the right amount of sunlight, but they always end up bedraggled and brown and eventually die, in spite of my best efforts. Equally, gardening is not something I am good at (or, if I'm truly honest, particularly motivated to do). Our garden tends to be looked after on a needs-must basis – usually when the needs are long overdue! This spring, as I tackled the lawn, I had to battle with brambles and cut back bushes that were trying to take over. The mowing of the lawn that should have taken about half an hour took much longer because we hadn't been vigilant in keeping the uninvited weeds under control. This is certainly no harmonious relationship!

Having said that, to sit in the garden in the sunshine, when the lawn is freshly cut and the trees and bushes are neatly trimmed, is a real joy. Our garden is a gift from God, and I love the opportunity to enjoy His creation in our small corner.

The phrase 'by the sweat of your face' (verse 19) is said to be an ancient Near Eastern idiom that speaks of anxiety and fear – sweat-inducing fear. So it doesn't just mean that humanity will from now on need to work hard just to have enough to get by; it is not just about sweating as a result of physical work. It also suggests that life will be characterised by ongoing insecurity, fear and worry – worry that our efforts won't be good enough, fear of events and circumstances beyond our control, and work-related stress.[4] Sleepless nights, worry about whether we can pay the bills this month, fears about job security, anxiety about our work performance, the feeling of not having enough control over our life and our future: all can bring us out into a cold sweat. And all are a result of the Fall. We will look further at this in chapter 6 when we look at the tree of Possessions.

We are not told how much time passed between creation and the Fall, but I am sure it would have been long enough for Adam and Eve to have experienced the full bliss of the paradise that was the Garden of Eden. There had been no striving. Their relationships with God, with one another and with the earth they were stewarding had been harmonious and free from tension and stress. There had been no sickness, no pain, no death, no decay. They would have known exactly what they had lost.

Notes

1 *Strong's exhaustive concordance.*
2 Sandra L. Richter, *The epic of Eden* (Downers Grove: IVP, 2008), p.109.
3 Andrew Perriman, 'He shall rule over you', 30th January 2012, from P.OST: An Evangelical Theology for the age to come. Available at: http://www.postost.net/2012/01/he-shall-rule-over-you (accessed 10th August 2014).
4 Richter, *The epic of Eden*, p.111, citing Daniel Fleming of New York University, 'By the sweat of your brow'.

Chapter 4
'We need a new plan'

They heard the sound of the Lord God walking in
the garden at the time of the evening breeze, and
the man and his wife hid themselves from the
presence of the Lord God among the trees of the
garden. But the Lord God called to the man and
said to him, 'Where are you?'
Genesis 3:8-9

Human beings were the pinnacle of God's creation, the crowning glory. Made in His image and according to His likeness, they were the special ones – the favourites, perhaps we could say, of everything He had made. Human beings were created to be God's special friends – and we betrayed Him. Betrayal by someone close, by a special friend, by someone in whom we have put our trust, cuts very deep. The closer the relationship, the deeper the hurt.

Part of being made in God's image and likeness, as we saw earlier, is that we are created with feelings and emotions, so this, of course, means that God experiences emotions too. He would have felt the pain of the man and the woman's betrayal and the anguish of their disobedience. When we are hurt and betrayed, our instinctive reaction is to protect ourselves and to turn away from the betrayer. Very often we elect to terminate the relationship, depending on the seriousness of the betrayal. Sometimes we even choose to shut out other people too, as a preemptive strike, to protect ourselves in case they betray us as well. Yet this was not God's reaction. Instead of choosing self-protection and retreating to lick His wounds, God reached out to the human beings.

So Adam and Eve were running away, trying to hide from God, and they had made clothing for themselves out of fig leaves. The consequences of their sin were serious, yet God, in His mercy and grace, chose not to leave humanity to live for ever in the mess they had made. He needed a new plan, and His Rescue Plan for humankind is the story that is told throughout the rest of the Bible. But this was a long-term plan, and it took thousands of years to bring it to fruition.

In the meantime, back in the garden, God had to deal with the immediate problem, which was to help Adam and Eve to come out of their hiding place. So He made clothes for them to help them to cover up their shame and embarrassment at their nakedness: 'And the Lord God made garments of skins for the man and for his wife, and clothed them' (Genesis 3:21).

How gracious God is! And how flexible! God could have told Adam and Eve that they had to remain naked because that had been His original plan – like it or lump it! But He is compassionate and loving, and He works with us through our mess-ups and helps us to find solutions when it all goes pear-shaped. Even though there were serious consequences for Adam and Eve, and even though they only had themselves to blame, God didn't abandon them and leave them to cope on their own. He gave them these clothes, firstly to help them to come out of their hiding place of shame, and secondly to protect them in and equip them for the new circumstances in which they were about to find themselves.

I love the fact that God made clothes for Adam and Eve. They had fashioned primitive clothes for themselves, out of fig leaves, but God made far superior clothes for them out of animal skins. He could have left them to wear their makeshift leaf-clothes but, in another example of His extraordinary flexibility and generosity, He gave them a gift of something far more comfortable and practical. And He still does this for us today – He helps us and equips us with what we need – even when we have messed up.

Yet it is also tremendously sad that this was necessary. Because of the man and the woman's sin, blood was shed. This had never been part of God's original plan for His creation, and it is another way in which death entered into the world. It would not be the last time blood would be spilt as a result of humanity's sin. Much more would need to be shed to deal with sin and its consequences, to enable human beings to come out of their hiding places, and ultimately to enable them to be restored to relationship with God.

When God went for His evening walk in the garden, Adam and Eve were nowhere to be seen. Now, I have no doubt that God, being omniscient, would have known exactly what had been going on during the day. He knew what they had done. But, again, in His graciousness, He still wanted to walk with them and to share company with them. When they hid from Him, He didn't walk away from them and leave the garden. He called out to them, 'Where are you?' The conversation then continued in a very gentle way. God at no time made accusations, but He calmly asked the man and the woman what had happened, and gave them every opportunity to tell Him. We note, too, that He gave them both an opportunity to speak and didn't just take the word of one over the other.

We need to take note here of who it is that turns away and hides. Sin has entered the garden and has brought with it the separation of humanity from God – they are no longer able to enjoy the intimate relationship they had with Him before. Yet God still loves the people He has created. He still longs for the companionship of human beings, and despite the pain of being betrayed, He is there to help them cope with the fallout and consequences of their actions. He begins to put in place His Rescue Plan for humanity, so that all people would have the opportunity to be restored to relationship with Him. But God does not remove our free will, and it is up to us to choose whether or not we wish to be reunited with Him.

God never stops loving us, and He never stops pursuing us, because He wants to rescue us and help us deal with the consequences of our sin, no matter what we have done, or where we are trying to hide, or how far we have tried to run away. God wants to remove the separation that our sin has brought; He wants to bridge the divide.

God comes looking for us, just as He went looking for Adam and Eve in the garden. He asks us, 'Where are you?' This is not because He does not know where we are – of course He does: He is God! But He wants us to acknowledge to ourselves where we are, to admit what we have done, and to ask for His help. Only when we acknowledge our need can we allow ourselves to be helped. We choose to hide among the trees, but God wants us to come out from there. He will give us clothes to wear to enable us to cope with whatever situation we find ourselves in, just as He gave Adam and Eve the clothes they needed to cope with their new circumstances. He meets us where we are, and leads us forward from that place. God does not expect us to make it to a certain point on our own before we can meet with Him. All we need to do is to acknowledge that we have created the divide, to recognise that our sin has built a barrier, and He will come to wherever we are and knock down all that stands in the way of our being restored to relationship with Him.

Writer and speaker Brad Jersak conveys this beautifully through 'The gospel in chairs', which is available on YouTube. He explains how God has continually pursued human beings throughout history, and is still pursuing us today. I would encourage you to watch it. Whenever we turn away, whenever we take a wrong turn, God follows us, waiting for us to take His hand and to ask Him to lead us back to His path again.

It's rather like being lost en route to a particular destination. First we have to acknowledge that we are lost. If we refuse to admit that we are lost, we cannot be helped, and we will ignore any directions anyone dares to attempt to give us – and likely get quite cross with them in the process! But once we admit that we don't know where we are, we can ask for directions and are in a position to accept help. God is always there, waiting to be asked, but He won't force Himself upon us. When we ask Him, He will take us by the hand and show us the way again. Sometimes we need to work out where, why and how we went wrong, otherwise we might take the same wrong turning again, and make the same mistake. Again, if we ask Him, God will help us work it out.

We will look in a bit more detail about some of the ways we can do this in chapter 11. For now, let me just say that God knows our heart, and He knows when we want to ask for His help. Perhaps it feels too difficult sometimes even to pray, or to read the Bible. Perhaps we feel that we really aren't good enough for God to listen to us, or that we have strayed too far from the path for Him to bring us back. Please be assured that God never has and never will stop loving you. Psalm 139 reminds us that there is not a single place we can go to where God does not pursue us:

> Where can I go from your spirit?
> Or where can I flee from your presence?
> If I ascend to heaven, you are there;
> if I make my bed in Sheol, you are there.
> If I take the wings of the morning
> and settle at the farthest limits of the sea,
> even there your hand shall lead me,
> and your right hand shall hold me fast.
> *Psalm 139:7-10*

Hiding among the trees

Adam and Eve tried to hide from God among the trees in the garden. God knew exactly where they were, but they needed to acknowledge the mistake they had made so that God could meet them there and help them. God never forces Himself upon anyone; when He made us He gave us free will, and although the invitation is always there, and He longs for us to accept it, He will never force us to follow Him. He wants us to love Him out of choice, not like automatons, who just follow a set of encoded instructions and are not able to think for themselves.

As I mentioned in the introduction, I spent a lot of my life hiding away from other people. I felt that I was not good enough and that people would not like me if they got to know the real me. I would wish I was like this person, or that person, because they were popular, or confident, or artistic, or sporty, or... and so the list goes on. What it took me far too long to realise was that God had made me to be an individual, and He loves the person He created me to be. He created me for a purpose, and that purpose is unique to me and my life. It is not the same as His purpose for anybody else's life. I began to realise that by wishing I was like someone else, I was actually denying, even disrespecting, what God had created. He created me, but by being dissatisfied with who I was, I was effactually saying that He had not done a very good job, that what He had made was rubbish.

Of course, the person I am today has been tainted by sin, and I realise that I am not the person God originally intended me to be when He first created me, as His image and likeness within me have been damaged and distorted. Yet He is still pleased with me and loves me completely. Who am I to disagree with God?!

I believe we all hide ourselves away, to a greater or lesser extent. Perhaps this is necessary – to a point. There are times when we need to hide ourselves from certain people and from certain situations for our own protection. But we should not be hiding all the time, and that's what I was doing. I am not saying I have it all sussed now – far from it. I know I still have a long way to go, but I am realising that God loves me unconditionally. I am learning to come out of my hiding places. I am even learning to take risks because I know that God is always with me, holding my hand, and He will always look after me and – as long as I listen to Him – He will show me the right way to go.

Adam and Eve tried to hide from God among the trees, and they used fig leaves to hide from each other. Today we use different hiding places, and in the next few chapters we will explore some of these 'trees'– the six Ps – we try to hide behind, from God and from each other.

We will also look at Jesus and the way He lived when He was on earth, and to explore how He was able to live His earthly life without hiding. Jesus, as we saw earlier, is the perfect, unmarred image of God, and we can do no better than to look to Him for a blueprint of how to live our lives.

The first 'tree' we will look at is the tree of power.

Chapter 5
The first tree: Power

But the serpent said to the woman, 'You will not
die; for God knows that when you eat of it your
eyes will be opened, and you will be like God,
knowing good and evil.'
Genesis 3:4-5

At the time of writing, my stepson and his fiancée are expecting
a baby in about a month's time – a little girl. I know without a
doubt that she will be welcomed into a very loving home, and
she will have parents (not to mention grandparents!) who will
love her to pieces! I also know, however, that that little girl will
rule the roost, at least for a while, and her every cry, her every
need, her every want, will be catered for. No matter what time
of the day or night, no matter how exhausted Mum and Dad
might be, she will cry, and they will answer the summons.

Babies are helpless creatures, unable to do very much at all
for themselves, yet they exert tremendous power. And it isn't
only when they cry. Many people, when they see a newborn
baby, will become all mushy inside – me included! Babies and
little children appeal to something deep inside us – a caring,
nurturing, protective instinct. The first time they smile, the first
time they laugh, the first time they crawl, or stand up, or walk,
or when their first tooth comes through, or when they say their
first word – all these occasions are received with much joy, and
everyone must be told! It's compulsory!

As babies grow and become toddlers and older children, they
need to learn that it isn't right for them to hold all the power, and
much of the power they are able to exert when they are babies

will gradually be taken away from them. They will learn that their every whim will not be met with a positive response, and sometimes the answer to their request will be 'No' or 'Wait'. They will begin to understand the difference between 'needs' and 'wants': their needs, of course, must be attended to, but their wants might not always be. Indeed, what they want might not be good for them. (I'm sure every child would *want* to eat the whole bag of sweets all at once – and perhaps some adults too!) They have to learn to live by the rules, for their own benefit, for the benefit of the rest of the family and for the good of wider society. Yet they will always have an element of power, and this is only right.

My children are growing up fast – they are now 18, 16 and 12. They have learned (even if they have to be reminded at times!) the rules of the household, and they respect them. They know that there is a certain hierarchy in the house, and that the rules are there not because we want to spoil their fun, but because they make for a household that is harmonious and that runs smoothly. They also know that certain rules are for their protection and well-being. Yet there is room for negotiation, and that is a good thing. As parents, my husband and I realise that we are not infallible, and we don't rule the roost with an iron rod, daring anyone to challenge decisions we have made or things we have spoken. We welcome calm and reasoned discussion if there is a difference of opinion. We have even been known to change our minds on occasion! Our children are able to influence the way things happen in the home – they have *power* to change and affect things. It is important for everyone – including children – to feel that they have a voice, that their opinion is welcomed and respected. Denying someone this voice can do a lot of damage to their self-esteem and confidence. As we observed earlier, touch, affection and love are critical to a child's personal development.

Power is something we all have, to a greater or lesser extent, within our spheres of influence, whether it be our homes and families, our friendship groups, our workplace, our church, or another group we are a part of. This is healthy and natural.

Some people within certain groups naturally have more 'power' than others. As parents, my husband and I have more power within the family unit. The manager of a department in the workplace will have more power than those who report to him or her. A school teacher has more power within the classroom than the pupils, but less power than the head teacher. Within a friendship group there might be a natural leader, one who is looked up to because they are considered to make wise decisions, for example. Depending on the type of church we go to, some of the leadership might be considered to have more power than the rest of the members or regular attenders; other churches advocate 'every person ministry', where decisions are made by the body as a whole.

Power becomes a problem when it becomes an end in itself, or when we use it for our own benefit rather than for the benefit of others. We can use our power to exert authority and to manipulate situations to our own ends. We all do it, whether we are aware of it or not. From the small child who flutters her eyelashes and smiles sweetly at her daddy because she knows he will give in to her demands, to the departmental manager who throws his weight around because he wants things done a certain way, with no regard for whether or not it is the best thing for the rest of the team or for the organisation as a whole, we can all 'do' something to get our own way.

When it is used in this way, power becomes a hiding place – when we do something to influence a situation in order to achieve a particular result, or for our own ends. We might throw our weight around in order to exert control over a person or a situation because we feel we would be unable to cope with a different outcome, or perhaps for entirely selfish reasons. Feelings of insecurity mean we might try to manipulate a situation to make it feel more comfortable rather than having to face our insecurities and fears. We use the authority we have in a situation or a relationship to influence the outcome, or the other person's behaviour, rather than seeking to develop and deepen relationships so that we can work together to find solutions and to grow together.

We hide behind our power and influence because we fear the intimacy of relationships, or because we fear we might lose control of the way things are done. We think our way is best and feel threatened if that is questioned. But by working together, by admitting that we don't have all the answers and we don't always know best, we might surprise ourselves. The solutions we find together are often so much better than what we are able to come up with on our own.

When my eldest son was about 14, he wanted to go out on Tuesday evenings to Soul Survivor cell group meetings. (Soul Survivor is a church in Watford with a strong youth contingent, led by Mike Pilavachi.) My immediate reaction was no, he would be out too late and he would be coming home on his own in the dark, and that worried me too much. I could see by the look on his face that he was disappointed, but he accepted and respected my decision.

As I thought about this and chatted it through with my husband, I began to realise that the reason I had said no was because of my own fears and insecurities. I was worried that something might happen to him as he travelled on public transport late in the evenings. I realised that I was using the power I had within the relationship to keep things the way they were, because I felt comfortable with that. I wanted to wrap my son up in cotton wool and keep him safe. I began to think about some of the other things a 14-year-old boy might want to be doing with his evenings, and here I was trying to stop my son going to a church event and drawing closer to God!

Once I realised that I was hiding behind this power and using it for my own agenda, I changed my mind and told my son he could go to the meetings. He was very happy, and he has always respected my wishes that he let me know if he is going to be late home. He is now 18 and working as a sound and lighting technician at live events, so I won't even mention the times he gets home on occasions! Yes, I worry about him when he is out until silly o'clock in the morning – I wouldn't be normal if I didn't – but I entrust him to God, go to bed and do my best to go to sleep! I have to realise that, in order for him to flourish and grow as an independent human being, I need to let go of the control and allow him to make his own decisions and his own way in the world. Of course, I will always be here for him when he needs me – that goes without saying – but by exerting too much control, I would be preventing him from reaching his potential and becoming the person he has been created to be.

Scientia potentia est

'Knowledge is power', as Sir Francis Bacon is alleged to have said. And the book of Proverbs says:

> The wise prevail through great power,
> and those who have knowledge muster their strength.
> *Proverbs 24:5 (NIV UK)*

Knowledge is believed to give us advantages over others. A good education is considered to give children the best possible start in life and to maximise their opportunities for a good job and career prospects. We use information to our advantage – whether through 'the system' by passing exams and gaining qualifications, or by using what we know to influence situations and work them to our own ends.

Adam and Eve were tempted by the power of knowledge when the serpent said to them, 'your eyes will be opened, and you will be like God, knowing good and evil' (Genesis 3:5). At the time, they probably had no concept of what 'good' and 'evil' even were, although they were fully aware of what they had been told not to do. They knew that God knew everything, and they knew that God had ultimate power, so I guess it stood to reason that if they had the knowledge that God had, it would give them more power. And the temptation was too hard to resist.

But it all went horribly wrong. Yes, they received the desired knowledge, but, as we saw earlier, they were unable to cope with it – as God had known all along. This new knowledge didn't actually give them any more power, and they would now have to fight to regain even some of the authority that they had originally been given. They had been tasked with working and stewarding the earth in a loving, nurturing relationship, but now, as well as having to leave the paradise garden, they would have to struggle and sweat even just to source their basic needs.

All through history, humanity has fought and struggled with the earth to bring it under control. Long gone is the harmonious relationship we had with the earth at the time of creation. We are realising now that we have to respect the earth and give back to it, not bleed it dry of its resources and upset its natural balance, otherwise the human race will be in a lot of trouble in years to come.

Our natural tendency as human beings is to try to take control, especially when things are not going the way we would like them to. When they are not going our way, we can almost resort to dictator-like tendencies to try to get our own way and regain that control. What we must be aware of, of course, is our motivation. Am I wanting to exert control just because things aren't going the way I want them to? Is what I want really the best thing for everyone concerned? Is it the best possible solution? We need to work out what the real problem is, and then work out the best way forward – for everyone concerned; not just for ourselves.

Who am I?

We often identify ourselves by what we 'do'. When we meet someone for the first time, how do we introduce ourselves? Presumably we will tell each other our name; then, as often as not, we will chat about what we do – our job, perhaps an ability we have (whether we are a musician, an artist, a footballer, and so on), or perhaps a ministry we are involved in. We feel that what we do gives us status and influence; it defines who we are. If I have an 'important' job, that makes me an important person, therefore people will listen to me – I will have authority and power. If I have an important ministry, that means I must be a spiritual person with lots of knowledge and wisdom, so people will look up to me and respect me. Consciously or subconsciously, we think that what we do makes us who we are.

Years ago, a person's surname would help to identify who they were and offer information about them and their family. Many surnames told what people did for a living – Smith, Wright, Carpenter, Butcher, Baker, and so on. In Scotland and Ireland, boys would have the prefix Mac (or Mc) or O' to their surname, followed by their father's name, to indicate which family they belonged to. Some names would have been given to describe particular characteristics, such as Strong, Wise, or Black or White to describe hair colour. Indeed, a number of biblical characters were given new names by God, to go with their new role or responsibility: Abraham, Israel, Peter and Saul, for example. Other names told where people came from. Our own surname, Copeland, comes from Copeland in Cumbria, and I understand the name comes from the Old Norse *kaupland*, meaning 'bought land'. I must pay the place a visit sometime.

Nowadays, of course, our names give no clue as to what we do for a living, or about our characteristics or where we come from. We might give nicknames, though, appropriate to personality traits or looks. When my daughter was little, I sometimes called her Boo, because she looked just like the little girl out of the film *Monsters, Inc.*, with her big brown eyes and her dark hair in cute bunches.

Names and job titles, though, tell us very little about who a person really is. We might learn which family someone comes from and what they do for a living, but they tell us nothing about the person's character and personality. Certain names or titles might command respect – people might speak differently to a minister or a priest, for example – and how would we respond if we were to meet royalty? But these are just external trappings – they don't tell us who the person is in the eyes of God. In the eyes of God, all people are equal. He loves each and every person the same, and God takes no notice of job titles.

Many years ago I had the opportunity to meet His Royal Highness the Prince of Wales. I was managing a stand at a 'Britain in Morocco' exhibition in Casablanca for the company I was working for, and he came to visit the exhibition. I remember having quite conflicting feelings about it: I was nervous because he is an important man, yet there was also a part of me that was telling me he is no different from anyone else – he just happens to have a title because of the family he was born into. I also remember wrestling with the fact that I was told I would have to bow or curtsey. Apart from the fact I didn't even know how to curtsey (I am not blessed with such ladylike graces!), it didn't sit comfortably with me that I should bow to another human being, when the only one to whom I want to bow the knee is God Himself.

In the end, I think I managed some kind of fudged combination of a bow, curtsey and handshake all rolled into one. I don't think His Royal Highness was particularly impressed.

This does lead me to consider, though, how people in positions of authority might use the power they are given, whether they are born into or it or elected to the role. The kings in the Old Testament were a real mixed bag: some used the power they had very wisely and led the people of Israel in the way God had ordained; others chose to walk a very different path.

Two particular examples are King Saul and King David. Both were anointed by God to lead the people of Israel, both were given great responsibility, and both made huge mistakes. The difference, however, was in the way they dealt with these mistakes. Saul took things into his own hands when things didn't turn out in the way he had expected, and blatantly disobeyed a clear instruction from God (1 Samuel 13:11-14; 1 Samuel 15:1-10). So God rejected him as king.

David also abused the power he had, by committing adultery with Bathsheba and having her husband killed so that he could take her for himself (2 Samuel 11). God sent the prophet Nathan to David to make him realise that he had done a terrible thing, and that God was displeased with him. David acknowledged that he had done a dreadful thing and confessed his sin to God, and God forgave him. There were consequences for David of his sin, however, and those consequences affected other people as well. David and all concerned had to come to terms with those consequences.

Yet Saul, too, repented and asked for forgiveness (1 Samuel 15:24-25). So why did God reject Saul as king and continue to bless David's kingship? 1 Samuel 16:7 tells us that 'the Lord does not see as mortals see; they look on the outward appearance, but the Lord looks on the heart'. I can only assume that as God looked at the hearts of Saul and David as they repented and confessed their sin, He saw in David true penitence and a willingness to humble himself and to change, and an earnest desire to be obedient to Him, but did not see the same humility and earnestness in the heart of Saul. So in spite of David's sinfulness, and even though he continued to make mistakes, David's heart continued to be after God's own heart (1 Samuel 13:14), and God was able to use him greatly.

What about Jesus?

So how did Jesus, the perfect image of God in humanity, identify Himself? What did He do when things weren't going His way? How did He respond? Did He exert His power to retain control?

One thing that is certain is that Jesus was always self-controlled. He never allowed His personal wants and desires to get the better of Him, and He never manipulated any situation for His own benefit. His concern was always for those around Him.

Jesus was immensely powerful. But He never used His power for His own ends. He was brilliantly clever with words, yet He never used them to belittle anyone. Neither did He just go along with the majority for the sake of an easy life. Jesus wasn't a people pleaser; He was a God pleaser.

As the Son of God, Jesus could easily have commanded respect wherever He went, from everyone He met. Many, of course, did love and respect Him, but many did not, and eventually these people wanted to kill Him.

How do we respond when we think people don't like us? I know I have a habit of doing everything I can to try to make people like me: there is an inbuilt need in me, as there is in all of us, to be liked and to feel accepted. If I feel that I am not liked, that must mean I am not a good person, that I am lacking in some way. It makes me doubt my worth.

Jesus did not allow Himself to be bothered by what other people thought of Him, and He did not try to find His identity in what He did, whether that was His work – most likely as a carpenter – or His ministry as a teacher and healer.

Before His ministry had even started, Jesus' identity was questioned. In the desert, immediately after His baptism, the devil tested Him: 'If you are the Son of God, command this stone to become a loaf of bread' (Luke 4:3). Are you really who you say you are? Prove it!

Jesus was also tempted by food, not fruit as Adam and Eve were, but bread. He had been fasting in the desert for 40 days by this time so He would have been feeling very hungry and weak. As a human being, Jesus was subject to the same physical needs as the rest of us. The devil often targets our basic human needs and desires; he knows where we are vulnerable. Jesus had the opportunity here not only to change His circumstances, but also to prove who He was – to prove His power. But He resisted the temptation. His response? 'It is written, "One does not live by bread alone"' (Luke 4:4).

Of course, there was so much more at stake here than just Jesus' physical hunger. But the point I want to make is that Jesus knew who He was, and God knew who He was, and Jesus didn't feel that He needed to prove it to anyone. He didn't have to *do* anything to prove who He was: He was secure in the knowledge that He was the Son of God, and that was enough for Him. It didn't matter to Him what the devil – or anyone else for that matter – thought of Him.

When I am faced with the temptation to prove that I am capable of doing a particular thing, or when I feel that I am being compared with someone else and don't want to be found wanting, it can be very hard to remember that I am a child of

God, and I don't have to *do* anything to prove myself. I am a daughter of God. You, too, are a son or a daughter of God, and we don't have to do anything to earn it or to prove it. We are loved and accepted just as we are.

Freedom in relationships

Jesus' security in the knowledge of who He was can also be seen by His remarkable humility. It meant He felt free to serve without worrying about having to maintain a particular image in the eyes of other people. In John 13 He had no qualms about washing the disciples' feet, because He knew that there was nothing He could do and nothing anyone else could do that could change who He was or take away His Sonship. This gave Him tremendous security and great freedom, as He had nothing He wanted to prove. This provides a stark contrast to the disciples, who argued about who among them was the greatest (Mark 9:34).

I would encourage you to rest in the knowledge that you are a son or daughter of God, and to allow Him to love you for who you are. Ask Him to help you to step out from behind this tree of power. And as you take His hand and begin to step out from this hiding place, remember that you don't have to do anything to earn God's love. You don't have to do anything to earn His acceptance. You don't have to do anything to earn His approval. You already have it. Take the hand He offers you and ask Him to help you to live secure in the knowledge that you are His child.

I would also encourage you to realise that, in the same way as we cannot earn God's love, we should not try to earn the love of other people. God loves us unconditionally, and we should live our lives as an act of worship to Him, so that everything we do flows from our gratitude for what He has done for us and out of our love for Him in return.

If we feel that we need to earn the love of another person, I would say we need to re-evaluate the relationship. Real love does not demand; it gives freely, and it receives what the other person wants to give. There is a big difference between receiving and taking in a relationship.

If someone loves you because of what you do for them, you may feel that you have an element of power and control because you are able to 'make' that person love you. However, the reality is that they are actually the one who is holding the power over you, because you feel obliged to behave in a certain way, otherwise you fear that their love will be withdrawn. The balance of power is weighted strongly in the other person's favour. I would say to you, very gently, please consider whether this person really loves you at all, or whether they are just loving themselves by manipulating you to do what they want you to do. In my opinion, this is self-satisfaction; it is not love. What are they offering to you to express their love for you? Is this the way you really want to be loved? What will happen if and when you can no longer give them what they want, perhaps through illness or other circumstances? Is this the way God loves you – for what you can do for Him?

I was once involved in a relationship like this. The person concerned led me to believe that they loved me, and that they would continue to love me if I did everything I could to please them. Foolishly, I went along with it, and for far too long. I did everything I could to make the person love me, and I thought for a while that they did love me. But it always felt as though whatever I did, it wasn't good enough. So I tried even harder. But nothing changed.

Eventually I came to recognise what was going on, but not before much damage had been done to my already low self-esteem and self-confidence. I realised that actually, the person didn't love me at all, in spite of all their words, and that they were really only interested in loving themselves. In the end I found the courage to cut loose from the relationship, and God in His grace and mercy put people around me who loved me for the person I am. These people were – and still are – willing to give to me without wanting anything in return. I still find it hard to receive love at times, and always feel that I ought to be giving something back, but I am realising that real love doesn't ask for anything in return. It gives freely, without counting the cost. And it welcomes and receives our love in return, if we choose to give it.

If this situation sounds familiar, I would really encourage you to pray and then to talk to the person about your concerns. Cite examples of real situations – it is difficult for anyone to dispute facts – and then describe how those occasions made you feel. Do everything you can to bring the relationship to a place of a more even balance of power. Cover it with prayer, and speak together with a wise and experienced third party if you are both willing.

Allow yourself to be loved for who you are, not for what you can give.

Power is something we all have, and indeed it is something we all need in order to flourish as human beings. But we can hide behind our power and use it for the wrong reasons. We should consider how we use our power, and ask God to help us to use it for the benefit of others, to help them to blossom and develop as people, and to enable them to reach their full potential. We are all made in the image and according to the likeness of God, and He has blessed every one of us with a task to carry out and a role to fulfil. And that role is different for each of us. Let us step out from behind this tree, drop this fig leaf, and use the power we have to help others grow and become the people that God created them to be!

Now to the second 'tree': the hiding place of material possessions.

Chapter 6
The second tree: Possessions

'Do not store up for yourselves treasures on
earth, where moth and rust consume and where
thieves break in and steal; but store up for
yourselves treasures in heaven, where neither moth
nor rust consumes and where thieves do not break
in and steal. For where your treasure is, there your
heart will be also.'
Matthew 6:19-21

I recently bought a tablet device. It is one of those Windows hybrid mini-laptop/tablets. I've wanted one for a while but I haven't been able to justify the expenditure. But I have now come to the point where I think I can justify my 'need'. For the occasions when I need to take it with me to a meeting, it will be very handy, as my day-to-day working laptop is quite large and heavy. Carrying the large laptop around the supermarket because I am doing the weekly shop on the way home and don't want to risk leaving it in the car is quite inconvenient, and it makes my shoulder ache!

Do I really need a tablet? Probably not. Could I manage without it? Certainly. I have managed for long enough without it. But it will make my life much easier.

How much of my decision to buy this device was driven by need, and how much by want, by the desire to 'keep up' with what everyone else has? If I'm honest, probably a bit of both.

There is tremendous pressure on us today to have 'stuff'. Whether it's the latest tablet device, smartphone, games console, widescreen television, car, house, clothes, or whatever, we don't want to be left behind. We have an image to maintain, and having the right 'stuff' helps us to convey the right impression. We want other people to think we're doing OK, that life is good, and we know that this assessment is often based on material possessions.

Our culture tells us that we can – and, indeed, that we *should* – have it all. We work hard: we deserve it. We are led to believe that we can only be happy if we have the latest gadget or fashion accessory. When our friends talk about their new phone, or the new car they have just bought, or the holiday they have just booked, or we see their lovely new clothes, it can be difficult not to feel envious. Maybe we are unable to join in the conversation about the latest techno-gadgets or the current popular holiday destinations.

How does this make us feel? We might feel left out, even inadequate. Perhaps we think it is unfair – we work just as hard as they do, so why can't we afford all these things too? Maybe we feel a little resentful, and we start to feel dissatisfied with our lot in life. We don't want to be left behind or excluded.

Such feelings, I believe, are responsible for many of the credit card and other debts that people have. I also believe they are a very significant contributory factor in the recent rise in the use of so-called 'payday loan' companies. We may not be able to afford these things, but the message conveyed is that there is no need to worry – we can go to one of these payday loan companies and borrow what we need until payday, and then we can pay it back. Problem solved!

Only the problem isn't solved. The problem becomes bigger, because when payday comes, we still have to meet all our usual bills and expenses, and on top of it all we have this loan to pay back, plus the interest. This leaves us a bit short this month, so we borrow again – a bit more this time – until the next payday.

And then we owe more, and the interest grows, and the amount we owe keeps increasing. Before we know it, we are in a downward spiral of mounting debt.

The advertising these companies use is very clever. It appeals to the wants and desires in us all for more material possessions, for more luxury and comfort, and more of the 'good' things in life, and it sucks us right in. It has us believing that our life will be second-rate unless we have all these things, and that we can't possibly be happy without them. We live in a world that demands instant gratification, and which offers us the means to achieve it. Never mind how we're going to pay it back: what's important is that we are seen to have the right 'stuff' – and we need to have it *now*, before it goes out of fashion.

I recently saw an advert for a credit card. The wording was:

> You only live once ... At [name of credit card] we think
> that you deserve the best.

The message is clear: if you don't take advantage of this offer, life will pass you by and you'll be missing out.

The other problem with this need for 'stuff' is that it is impossible to keep up. As soon as we upgrade our phone, a new model is released. There is always a bigger house on the market, or a better, higher-performance car. Fashions change so quickly – we buy new clothes but they are out of date within a few weeks or months and discarded, many hardly worn. This constant changing means we never quite make it, and all this 'stuff' we accumulate never quite fills the hole we expected it to.

The culture we live in has a huge influence on our lives. It dictates what is acceptable, what is 'normal', what is expected of us. Today's Western society is highly consumerist – possibly more than ever before. We look around us and compare ourselves to the way we think others live, and we will always find people who have a lot more than we do. But when we look at the wider picture, we see that actually, we in the West are incredibly rich.

The world in miniature

The Miniature Earth Project has endeavoured to simplify statistics about the world's population by shrinking it to a village of just 100 people.[1] If we look at some of these statistics, it puts it all back into perspective and helps us to realise just how rich we in the West really are.

So, in the world shrunk down to a village of 100 people, keeping the same proportions:

- 51 live in urban areas

- 15 are hungry or undernourished

- 7 have an educational degree

- 14 live with some form of disability

- 20 people own 75 per cent of the village income

- 37 lack access to adequate sanitation

- 30 are active users of the internet

- 48 live on less than US $2 per day, and 80 live on less than US $10 per day[2]

If you have a fridge to keep your food in, a wardrobe to hang your clothes in, a bed to sleep in and a roof over your head, you are richer than 75 per cent of the world's population.

These are sobering statistics. I cannot help but be challenged about the things I deem to be important, when three-quarters of the people in the world don't even have what we would consider to be very basic necessities. Three-quarters of the world's wealth is owned by one-fifth of the people, and nearly half of the people in the world are struggling to get by on less than £1.30 per day to meet all of their needs.

Check your sources

This leads me to consider where many of the things we buy actually come from. How many of the clothes we wear have been manufactured by people in appalling conditions, or perhaps even by slaves?

It is estimated that 8.4 million children worldwide are in slavery, debt bondage or other forced labour, trafficking, prostitution or other illicit activities. It is also estimated that 1.2 million children are trafficked every year – that's more than 3,000 every day. Let me repeat that: more than 3,000 children are trafficked *every day*. Between 600,000 and 800,000 people are trafficked internationally each year, around 80 per cent of whom are women and girls. The figures are difficult to quantify because of the hidden nature of the activity, but it is said to be the fastest-growing global crime.[3]

But hasn't slavery been abolished? How can this still be happening? Well, sadly, trafficking is very lucrative – it is reckoned to be the second largest source of illegal income worldwide (exceeded only by drugs trafficking). Like many lucrative activities, when it is outlawed, it doesn't stop; it simply goes underground.

There are any number of different ways that people can end up in forced labour or being trafficked, but poverty is obviously the overriding cause. This then plays out in many different scenarios. In some areas work is scarce, so people will take any job they can find and end up working horrendously long hours for pitiful pay. Others will travel abroad following a false promise of work, only to find that their passport is taken to be 'looked after', and they end up enslaved until they can 'repay their debt' to the person who paid their fare. Still others feel they have no choice but to sell their children as they can no longer afford to feed them. Given hope by the false promise that their children will have the chance of a better way of life, they sell them – into a life of slavery, forced labour, prostitution or even child sacrifice.

Stop the Traffik tells of a family in Mumbai, India, who had no home and lived on a train station. A man offered the parents money for the two children, who were aged seven and nine. They were sold for the equivalent of US $30, and never seen or heard of again.[4]

And the issue is not just an international one. A recent report by the Salvation Army states that they have supported more than 1,800 victims of human trafficking in England and Wales since 2011.[5] These are just those who have received support – how many continue to be under the radar, still not known about?

So what can we do? The problem is huge. How can we possibly make a difference? Well, to begin with, we can try to find out where the clothes we wear and the food we eat comes from. We can buy fairly traded food whenever possible (look out for the Fairtrade mark in the supermarket), and check the websites of clothes manufacturers for their ethical trade policy. We can support organisations that are working to free those in slavery and to improve working conditions, and to prevent others from being drawn in. Child sponsorship programmes are another way in which children are being freed from the cycle of poverty.

God is passionate about justice, and in so much of the Bible – both the Old and New Testaments – we see that God's heart is for the poor, the widows and the orphans, for those who do not have a voice to speak up for themselves. Here are just a couple of examples:

> Learn to do good;
> seek justice,

rescue the oppressed;
defend the orphan,
plead for the widow.
Isaiah 1:17

'Woe to you, scribes and Pharisees, hypocrites! For you tithe mint, dill, and cummin, and have neglected the weightier matters of the law: justice and mercy and faith. It is these you ought to have practised without neglecting the others.'
Matthew 23:23

Indeed, God's people are told to actively favour the poor and the vulnerable. Isaiah was just one of the prophets who preached a strong message of justice and righteousness. Every person is expected to do what they can on a daily basis to help those in need: to feed the hungry, to shelter the homeless, to clothe those who are naked, to free the oppressed, and so on (Isaiah 58:6-7). It is not the responsibility of the leaders alone. It is a message that Jesus strongly reiterated (Matthew 25:31-46).

We might not feel that we can do very much, but we have a responsibility to do what we can. Every person on the face of the earth has been created in the image and according to the likeness of God. We are to love and respect that image in everyone we meet, and one way we can do that is to minister to people's needs. By doing so, says Jesus, we are ministering to Him. If we neglect to do what we can to help those in need, we bypass opportunities to minister to Jesus Himself (Matthew 25:40, 45).

What about Jesus?

What was Jesus' response to the temptation to accumulate 'stuff'? The first thing to notice is that Jesus was homeless. In Matthew 8:20 He says, 'Foxes have holes, and birds of the air have nests; but the Son of Man has nowhere to lay his head.'

As a young man, Jesus is likely to have learned His father Joseph's trade of carpentry, and presumably this is how He earned His living until He began His ministry. At the age of around 30, He gave it all up to become an itinerant preacher and healer, reliant on the hospitality of friends for a bed for the night, for food, and for all His material needs. We are told that a number of women 'provided for them out of their resources' (Luke 8:3). Mark tells us that a number of women 'used to follow him and provided for him when he was in Galilee' (Mark 15:41). He would stay at the home of Simon Peter and his family, or with His friends Mary, Martha and Lazarus in Bethany.

So Jesus was dependent on other people for His basic material and physical needs. And at times when there wasn't enough food to go around, God miraculously provided! Five loaves and two small fish fed 5,000 people (or perhaps, more realistically, 10–15,000 people by the time you include all the women and children); seven loaves and a few small fish fed more than 4,000 (Matthew 14:13-21; 15:32-38). And there were even leftovers!

Let's take a look at what Jesus said about money and possessions:

> As he was setting out on a journey, a man ran up and knelt before him, and asked him, 'Good Teacher, what must I do to inherit eternal life?' Jesus said to him, 'Why do you call me good? No one is good but God alone. You know the commandments: "You shall not murder; You shall not commit adultery; You shall not steal; You shall not bear false witness; You shall not defraud; Honour your father and mother."' He said to him, 'Teacher, I have kept all these since my youth.' Jesus, looking at him, loved him and said, 'You lack one thing; go, sell what you own, and give the money to the poor, and you will have treasure in heaven; then come,

follow me.' When he heard this, he was shocked and went away grieving, for he had many possessions.

Then Jesus looked around and said to his disciples, 'How hard it will be for those who have wealth to enter the kingdom of God!' And the disciples were perplexed at these words. But Jesus said to them again, 'Children, how hard it is to enter the kingdom of God! It is easier for a camel to go through the eye of a needle than for someone who is rich to enter the kingdom of God.' They were greatly astounded and said to one another, 'Then who can be saved?' Jesus looked at them and said, 'For mortals it is impossible, but not for God; for God all things are possible.'
Mark 10:17-27

The young man in this story knew there was something else to be had: his wealth and possessions did not satisfy him. He was religious and obeyed all the rules, but he knew something was lacking. He may well have been searching for fulfilment all his life – he had kept all the commandments since he was young, but it was not enough. He was hungry for something more, and he knew Jesus had the answer. Jesus offered him the solution, but it was not the answer the young man had been hoping to receive. Jesus told him where he could find his identity – in the kingdom of God – but it meant breaking his attachment to his possessions.

Let me make it clear here that Jesus is not saying that it is wrong to be wealthy. What He is talking about is when our *attachment* to wealth and possessions takes over. If our yearning for material possessions is greater than our yearning for God, then there is something wrong. Our material possessions are a blessing from God, and we are to hold them loosely. All that we have belongs to Him, and He has given it to us as a blessing, to look after, to steward wisely and to use in His service and for the benefit of others.

Who owns whom?

Jesus also told a parable about a rich fool:

> Someone in the crowd said to him, 'Teacher, tell my
> brother to divide the family inheritance with me.' But
> he said to him, 'Friend, who set me to be a judge or
> arbitrator over you?' And he said to them, 'Take care!
> Be on your guard against all kinds of greed; for one's
> life does not consist in the abundance of possessions.'
> Then he told them a parable: 'The land of a rich man
> produced abundantly. And he thought to himself,
> "What should I do, for I have no place to store my
> crops?" Then he said, "I will do this: I will pull down
> my barns and build larger ones, and there I will store
> all my grain and my goods. And I will say to my soul,
> Soul, you have ample goods laid up for many years;
> relax, eat, drink, be merry." But God said to him, "You
> fool! This very night your life is being demanded of
> you. And the things you have prepared, whose will
> they be?" So it is with those who store up treasures for
> themselves but are not rich towards God.'
> *Luke 12:13-21*

The man in the crowd is asking Jesus to make a judgement. It
wasn't unusual at that time for rabbis to be asked to mediate in
such matters. And of course, the man wants a judgement in his
favour.

We don't know any of the details about this man's situation.
In the culture of that time the eldest son would inherit a double
portion – twice as much as any siblings he might have. This was
to reflect the extra responsibilities and duties he would be
expected to carry as the eldest son. Perhaps this man who comes
to Jesus is a younger son who feels that it is unfair that his older
brother has inherited twice as much as he has. Maybe his father
cut him off for some reason and now he has come to sniff out

what he feels is rightfully his share. We don't know. But whatever his situation, I think it's pretty safe to say he wants the security of material wealth.

In the first century, owning land was important to the Jews, for the obvious economic reasons, but also for religious reasons. God had made a promise to Abraham that God would give him and his descendants land, and continuing to own land was a way for them to hang on to this promise. Owning land meant security, and it was also seen as a sign of God's favour.

Verse 20 says, 'This very night your life is being demanded of you.' We generally assume from this that the man dies that night. And indeed that's a right and valid interpretation. We work hard to earn money so we can buy the things we need and live a comfortable life, but none of us knows how long we have left on this earth. We are reminded that, 'You can't take it with you', or, according to an Arab saying, 'There are no pockets in a shroud.' It is a point we would do well to remember.

Jesus follows this parable with a reassurance that we are not to worry – God has it all under control and will take care of all our needs:

> 'But if God so clothes the grass of the field, which is alive today and tomorrow is thrown into the oven, how much more will he clothe you – you of little faith! And do not keep striving for what you are to eat and what you are to drink, and do not keep worrying. For it is the nations of the world that strive after all these things, and your Father knows that you need them. Instead, strive for his kingdom, and these things will be given to you as well …
>
> For where your treasure is, there your heart will be also.'
> *Luke 12:28-31, 34*

Theologian Wayne Stacy suggests that the man in the parable in fact does not die; rather he lives and becomes a slave to his possessions. *They* own *him*. He suggests that a more literal translation of verse 20 of the parable might be 'Fool! This night *they* shall require your very life from you; now who owns whom?' (A Greek scholar I know says this is an unlikely translation, although not impossible. However, it is still a point that is well worth considering, so we'll go with it.)

Who are *they*? In the context of the passage, *they* are his 'things', his possessions, his 'stuff'.[6] The goods he has worked so hard for now dominate his life. He builds bigger barns to hold them all, and the chances are that he will now be lying awake at night, worrying that someone will slip in and steal them, or that something else untoward might happen to them. They become his obsession and dominate his thoughts, taking his focus off of God and the things of the kingdom.

The rich fool is not a fool because he is rich, but because he puts his trust in his possessions rather than in God. His focus is on himself and his own needs, rather than the kingdom of God. He is hiding behind the tree of material belongings. We only have to look at the number of times the words 'I', 'me' and 'my' are used in verses 17 and 18 to see where his priorities lie.

I have been trying to take this on board in my own life recently. In my head I know that everything I have belongs to God, but in my heart it is very hard to let go. I think of things as *mine* – *my* time, *my* money, *my* home – but instead I should be thinking of it as *God's* time, *God's* money, *God's* home, and asking Him what He wants me to do with them. Too often I do it the other way around – I make decisions about what I want to do, and ask God to bless my plans. Instead, I should be seeking what God is doing, and what He wants to do, and stepping in with Him. Let's face it – His plans are far better than anything I could come up with anyway!

I'll be honest with you here. There have been times in my life when things have been very tight financially. But at no time have I received a bill that I could not pay. Somehow, I have always had the money come in from somewhere so I could meet my financial commitments.

Our car recently had to be scrapped. It broke down with no prior warning, and there was so much wrong with it that it just wasn't worth repairing. I had had it for 12 years, and it had served me very faithfully. I bought it three weeks after my daughter was born, and over the years I had grown quite attached to it!

So here we were, two weeks before we were due to go on holiday, with no transport! Yet God's hand was so clearly visible in the whole process.

We had driven the best part of 120 miles that day, and we broke down just two miles from home. With the help of friends and family we were able to get ourselves home, and the car was towed to the mechanic in the hope it might be fixable. Sadly, it wasn't to be.

But God in His goodness had already provided the money we needed for a replacement car, completely unexpectedly and out of the blue! A couple of months earlier, my husband had received some money from an insurance policy that had matured that he had completely forgotten about. We had no idea the money was coming, and when it arrived we were amazed! We figured God must have something in mind for it – although we had no idea what – so we put it into a savings account. This money, plus a little extra that we were able to find, was enough for us to buy a car. We had a very limited budget, but we were able to find a very nice car with low mileage, without having to use any of the finance deals the car dealers were trying to persuade us to take out – we were adamant that we weren't going to borrow any money!

You would think these experiences would help me to trust God the next time things get tight, but I am a slow learner, sadly. I still stress and worry at times, yet God has never let us down.

Being self-employed and working freelance (my bread-and-butter job is as a copywriter, editor and proofreader, and I am also an author and speaker), there are times when work is a little thin on the ground. Fortunately that doesn't happen very often, I'm glad to say. When it does happen, I am always tempted to worry. When will the next job come in? What will I do if nothing comes in for weeks? How will we manage financially? Again, you would think I would have learned by now. But God always provides, and something always comes in, generally much sooner than I anticipate. And I have noticed that at times when I have little or no work, it is either because God wants to attract my attention for some reason, or because He wants to free up my time to do something else.

Three years ago I needed to make the decision whether to go full-time with my freelance business (which I had been doing for the previous eight years) or whether to continue to do the part-time job I had as well. It was a difficult decision as I loved my part-time job, but I was struggling to cope with everything I was doing and I knew something had to give. Circumstances meant I had to make a decision one way or another on a particular day. I was without any freelance projects at that time, which is perhaps quite ironic considering I was making a decision to do this full-time! Yet what might seem to be illogical in human terms is often the right thing in kingdom terms.

Deep down I knew what I needed to do, so I made my decision and handed in my notice the next morning. By midday the day after that, two fairly sizeable jobs had landed in my inbox. That was unusual in itself, as it was a Saturday, and it's quite uncommon for me to receive jobs over the weekend, especially from my regular clients who are all Monday to

Fridayers – and at least one of the jobs, as I recall, was from one of my regulars. To me, that was God's way of confirming that I had made the right decision.

God is the manager of my business, and He manages my workload, and I am very grateful that He does! When I do manage not to worry, it relieves me of an enormous burden!

Worry and fear

Worry is something we all face. Some of us worry more than others. Some people seem to be so laid back that nothing appears to faze them; others appear to worry so much about risk and potential consequences that they end up doing nothing at all.

I recently came across some statistics about worry. It is said that:

- Forty per cent of the things we worry about never happen – so in fact we're wasting our time and our energy worrying about them.

- Thirty per cent of what we worry about has already happened. We can't go back and change it, and can rarely do anything about it. I was in the car with my son recently and I was a little uptight because I had left later than I had intended to. He could see I was getting quite antsy so he said to me, 'Mum, why are you stressing? You can't change the situation and make it so that you left earlier, so why worry?' He was so right. I realised there was no point worrying. And my arrival at my destination wasn't even particularly time critical, anyway. Why was I wasting my energy?!

- Twelve per cent are unnecessary worries, such as what someone else thinks about us.

- Ten per cent are petty and unimportant such as what to have for dinner or what to wear.

So 92 per cent of our worries are either about things that are relatively unimportant or about things that we can't do anything to change. That's quite a lot. Imagine how it would be if we could eliminate 92 per cent of our worries. How liberating would that be?!

That leaves eight per cent of the things we worry about that are more significant and important, and which may actually happen. Of this percentage...

- Four per cent are things that are beyond our control, such as worries about our health, our loved ones or an impending natural disaster. Sometimes, the reality of these events is less difficult to deal with than the worry about them, although not always. Many of these things do affect us if and when they happen, and I am not for one second suggesting that because we cannot have any effect on them that we don't allow them any headspace – we are not robots without feelings. We might be hurt, angry, grieving or confused. And that's right and natural. God created us for relationships, and when something happens that affects us or affects someone we love, particularly when it's out of our control, it can be very hard to deal with. It is vital to acknowledge those feelings and deal with them. Sometimes that takes time, but we need to allow God to help us through, and let other people in to help us as well.

- The final four per cent of what we worry about we are said to have some, if not all, control over.[7]

Four per cent is not a lot, is it?

Recently my son moved into sixth form and had to decide whether to stay at his school or to move to a sixth-form college. It was a very hard decision for him to make. He had done well in his GCSEs at school and was very happy there; he had made good friends and he knew and liked all the teachers for the subjects he wanted to study for A level. But he also knew that the college has an excellent reputation, and he wanted to go there too. This was a situation over which he had some control, but he didn't know what the right decision was, and he worried about making the wrong one.

I was confident that he would do well whichever decision he had made; he is a hard worker and is motivated to study. But I fully understood his angst: he wanted to make the right decision to give himself the best chance of achieving the highest possible results.

In the end he decided to go to the sixth-form college. Fortunately he is very happy there and is still doing well and achieving good results. Long may it last!

I confess that I am a worrier. I worry about all sorts of things. I worry about the children and their safety, and about their future; I worry about my wider family and friends; I worry about safety and home security; I worry about finances, about work… I know in my head that I shouldn't worry, and I keep praying and giving it all to God, but it's easier said than done. I know worrying is not part of God's plan for us, and it was not part of His original blueprint for the creation of human beings.

God challenged me about this recently. I was away at a residential for my part-time Theology degree. In one of the lectures we were asked the question, 'What would you do if God asked you to give everything away?' Would I do it? Was I completely surrendered to Him? My initial reaction was to brush it under the carpet with the response that, yes, of course I am surrendered to Him. My life has taken some unexpected turns over recent years as I have taken steps of obedience to Him, therefore I must be surrendered. Mustn't I?

God, in His grace and wisdom, didn't let me off the hook quite that easily. He put the right person in my way at just the right time, who asked me just the right question. And I was forced to confront it: I couldn't hide behind the tree any more.

Thankfully God didn't ask me to give everything away – or, at least, He hasn't so far. But that day, as I wrestled with this issue, He gradually made me realise that He wanted to help me deal with something that had begun to take hold in my life: fear.

As I mentioned earlier, I spent many years struggling with low confidence and low self-esteem, and now I am in a place where I am, on the whole, happy being the person God has created me to be. Of course, I am a work in progress – no one knows that better than I do – but God is working on me.

A number of years ago I was released from a difficult marriage. At the time I never expected – or indeed, wanted – to be involved with anyone again, but God had other plans, and I am now happily married. I have three children who are a real blessing from God; I enjoy my work, my studies, my writing and speaking engagements. Life is not by any means without its challenges, but on the whole it is good, and I am happy and content with my lot.

Yet what God was gently pointing out to me that day was that fear had begun to take hold of me. Fear that the bubble would burst. Fear that it was too good to be true. Fear that something dreadful would happen and that it would all come crashing down around my ears.

I would love to be able to say that God promised that the garden would always be rosy, but that is not true; we all know that life is not like that. Struggles and difficulties will inevitably come. Being a Christian does not make us immune to difficult times. But what God did clearly say is that He is infinitely bigger than any problem I could ever face, and that His ability to bless me is far greater than the enemy's ability to curse me. He reassured me of His love, and that He will always be with me and will always guide me.

Worry and fear are thieves of peace and joy. They are not part of God's plan for us. And while we all have to deal with the struggles and the pain and the difficulties that life will inevitably throw at us, God is much bigger than they are, and He is more than capable of carrying us through the hard times.

Going back to the rich fool in Jesus' parable, what was it that prompted him to build these big barns in the first place? Fear, worry and anxiety about the future. He thought that building these barns and storing up goods for himself would provide him with security for his future and free him from stress. But the sad irony is that, instead of freeing him from worry and fear, he now has more to worry about, so he feels even more insecure than he did before! Instead of bringing him freedom, they have trapped him.

When we have wealth and possessions, we put our trust in them. That is perfectly normal and natural. We need money to buy food and clothes and to put a roof over our heads, and so on. It is not wrong to have possessions. But we need to make sure we get our priorities in the right order. God must take first place in our lives, then come our relationships with others, and at the bottom is our 'stuff'.

Jesus came to bring the kingdom of God to earth; not to bring wealth and possessions to people. He came to point us towards God, and to encourage us to be 'rich towards God' (Luke 12:21). This richness towards God is about our relationship with Him – a relationship of love, dependence and trust. The kingdom of God is the only true security we can have. We need to take His hand and step out from behind this tree of possessions. He wants us to let go of our attachment to our possessions and find our identity in Him. We are called to prioritise the kingdom of God in our lives. As we do this, we give God permission and room to begin to restore His image in us.

Let us remember that the material blessings we have received are a gift from God. He loves to bless His children, and He loves it when His children bless each other. Let us look out for each other and use our time and our possessions for the benefit of others, as well as to meet our own needs. God does not want us to focus our time, attention and energy on material wealth and possessions. His kingdom is much more important, and when we put His kingdom first, 'all these things will be given to you as well' (Matthew 6:33).

The world was created with more than enough resources for everyone if they were to be shared fairly. And God continues to sustain the earth, His creation, and to provide more than enough for the earth and all its inhabitants to survive and thrive. Human beings are the managers of the earth: it is up to us to administer its resources wisely and to ensure that they are shared fairly among the whole of humanity. Let us see the image of God in every human being, and seek to minister wherever we see need.

Am I focused on God's kingdom, or am I focused on my material wealth and possessions? What am I doing with the money and the 'stuff' that God has given me? Am I using it in the way He wants me to – to bless others who are not as fortunate as I am? What are we doing to support organisations who are working to ensure a more fair distribution of the world's wealth?

We'll have a look now at the third 'tree' we might hide behind – being busy, or the tree of productivity.

Notes

[1] The Miniature Earth Project uses data from the World Health Organization, WorldBank, Census, United Nations and others. See http://www.miniature-earth.com/ (accessed 6th May 2015).

[2] At today's exchange rate (6th May 2015) US $2 is equivalent to approximately £1.31, and $10 equivalent to approximately £6.55.

[3] Information taken from Stop the Traffik website: http://www.stopthetraffik.org/the-scale-of-human-traffiking (accessed 5th March 2015).

[4] From Stop the Traffik: http://www.stopthetraffik.org/ (accessed 20th October 2014).

[5] BBC News, 'More people trafficked for labour than sex trade, says report' 13th October 2014. Available at http://www.bbc.co.uk/news/uk-29591933 (accessed 20th October 2014).

[6] R. Wayne Stacy (Professor of Religious Studies, Gardner-Webb University, North Carolina), 'Luke 12:13-21: The parable of the rich fool', *Review and Expositor*, 94 (1997), 285-292.

[7] Cindy Holbrook, '12 techniques to stop worrying', 24th September 2008. Available at http://www.pickthebrain.com/blog/stop-worrying/#u7eJ8EAk4YwHLEGW.99 (accessed 7th March 2015).

Chapter 7
The third tree: Productivity

And on the seventh day God finished the work
that he had done, and he rested on the seventh
day from all the work that he had done. So God
blessed the seventh day and hallowed it, because
on it God rested from all the work that he had
done in creation.

Genesis 2:2-3

Why do we feel guilty when we're doing nothing in particular? We long to relax, perhaps to sit and read a book or watch a film, or even just to 'veg out' for a while. But we wrestle with feelings of guilt, and we think to ourselves, 'I ought to be *doing* something.'

We live in a culture that is driven by productivity, by the need to achieve. Working hours are becoming longer and even more results driven. There is emphasis in the workplace on setting and achieving targets, and these targets are becoming more stretching as time goes on. More is expected of us, in less time and with a smaller budget. Often, the only way to meet these goals is to spend more time working.

The cost of living seems to be going up at a rapid rate, yet our income isn't growing at the same speed. Sometimes the only way to make ends meet is to work longer hours. We may have the joy of a promotion, yet inside a part of us dreads the expectations we know will be upon us to work even longer hours and to hit even bigger targets.

This is the unfortunate reality for many in the West. To be honest, I'm not sure what the answer is. We are faced with the stark reality of having to pay the bills and to put food on the table, a roof over our heads and clothes on our backs. Many have no alternative but to work long hours to meet their financial commitments.

Economic hardship in recent years has forced many to re-evaluate their priorities and make drastic changes to the way they live their lives. Sadly, many are simply unable to manage financially. The rise in the use of foodbanks is testimony to that. The Living Wage Foundation was set up to encourage employers to pay a realistic living wage rather than just the minimum wage, as even some who work full-time are still living in poverty. Zero hours contracts haven't helped. As I write, the current minimum wage for those over the age of 21 is £6.50 per hour, yet the living wage rate for London is £9.15 per hour and £7.85 per hour for the rest of the UK. What a difference that £2.65 or £1.35 per hour would make to the wage packet at the end of the week or month![1]

Avoiding the elephant in the room

Life in the twenty-first century is very busy, there is no doubt about that. We have more labour-saving devices than any generation has had before us, yet we seem to have less free time.

Our dishwasher recently broke and we didn't replace it straight away. We were without one for about six weeks or so, and we all took our turn to do the washing-up. With the five of us all doing our fair share, it didn't really take up much of our time, but how relieved and happy we all were when the new dishwasher arrived! But what is it that we are all so desperate to get back to doing? Working? Studying? Watching television? Sleeping? I found myself feeling frustrated about having to do the washing-up after lunch because I was itching to get back to work (now God has blessed me with a full schedule!), yet it didn't really take that long. And I found that it gave me a few minutes to think and to ponder that I otherwise wouldn't have had. An additional bonus was that the hot water warmed my hands, which are always cold in the winter!

We must be careful that we are not hiding behind our busyness and using it to avoid facing some of the issues we might otherwise have to deal with. Do we hide behind our busyness because it gives us a sense of worth, and we feel that we are making a contribution and doing something of value with our life? We need to feel needed, and being busy gives us a sense of purpose. Perhaps this goes back to our need for power that we discussed in chapter 5. Being busy makes us feel important, and gives us the feeling that we have power and influence.

Sometimes being busy is actually the easy option: we might choose to be busy because it gives us an excuse to avoid some of the real issues we need to face. If we are occupied with something, we can avoid having to think about other things. It is easier to bury ourselves in our work, or perhaps our hobbies and pastimes, than to have a difficult conversation with a loved one about a particular matter. So we hide behind our busyness and brush the issue under the carpet.

The problem is that the issue doesn't go away. It grows and grows, until it becomes unavoidable. But by then it is so much more difficult to manage because it has grown out of all proportion. Time has allowed irritation and anger to fester, and what started out as a little pimple is now a fully grown, pus-filled boil. Getting rid of the boil is much harder work – and more painful – than it would have been to deal with the pimple when it first raised its head.

Perhaps we simply find it hard to say no when someone asks us to do something, and we feel that our busyness is not our fault because others are continually making demands on us. We might be struggling to fit everything in and it is taking its toll on our health. We are constantly tired because we don't take enough time to rest. It might be affecting our relationships because we aren't spending enough time with our loved ones. We might be feeling resentful about all the things we *need* to do and because we never have any time to relax and do the things we *want* to do, so everything we are involved in becomes drudgery. Life has lost its joy.

On the other hand, we might try to do everything ourselves because we don't want to be a burden to others. I find myself in this situation sometimes. I have a tendency to try to do everything in the house to save my husband having to do it. He works long hours and I want him to be able to rest when he comes home from work. But he is aware that I work long hours too, so he is keen to do his share – and he does a lot more than just his fair share. Because I work from home, I have the flexibility of being able to choose my working hours (to a point!), and I can work late into the evenings and over the weekends if necessary to make up for time taken out during the day or the week.

I am also aware that I don't have the ability to do everything! One of the lovely things about my relationship with my husband is the mix of skills we have. I tend to do the organising and the admin, and he is the practical one. If something breaks or needs putting together, I'm hopeless! I realise that I need to focus on the things that I am good at, and allow others to focus on the things they are good at. This is one reason why God made us to be relational beings and put us in families and communities – so we can help each other out and all make a contribution. It is also why He didn't give any one person the ability to do everything. They would have little need of anyone else, which would not be a healthy place to be, and they would likely end up burning out because they were doing everything and didn't take time to rest! Needing other people and having to ask for support occasionally also helps to keep us humble!

As we saw in chapter 1, part of God's image in us is that we were created as relational beings. As we each use our own particular strengths and allow others to use theirs, we are embracing the individual giftings and particular aspects of His image that He has chosen to place within us.

Busyness can be dangerous, too. Focusing too much time and energy on working and on always being busy doing things can have a detrimental effect on our relationships, not to mention our health. Relationships need the investment of time and energy – of our best; not just anything we happen to have left in the tank at the end of the day.

This applies even more to our relationship with God. If we are too busy to spend time with Him, how will we hear His voice when He tries to speak to us? And if we are not hearing His voice, how will we know what He wants us to be doing? It becomes all too easy to fall into doing the wrong things. These things may not even be 'sinful' things, although that is a possibility too, of course. It might just be that we begin to wander away from God's best plan for our lives.

What about Jesus?

So how did Jesus manage not to be bogged down with busyness? There were so many people clamouring for His time and attention and making demands on Him. How did He manage not to be constantly busy? How did He manage to always have the energy and compassion to help people, without feeling resentful that they were intruding on His time and space?

Jesus would often take time out to pray. He would go off by Himself just to spend time with His heavenly Father. Luke 5:16 tells us that Jesus 'would withdraw to deserted places and pray'. Mark 1:35 tells us that Jesus would do this 'in the morning, while it was still very dark'. I have to confess that this is a challenge for me. Anyone who knows me knows how I struggle to get out of bed in the mornings! Yet I acknowledge how important it is to spend time with my heavenly Father each day, and I make sure I have some time with Him every morning before the day begins.

People would pursue Jesus and would often seek Him out when He was having some 'alone' time. Yet He never turned them away. In Matthew 14, Jesus had just been told about the death of John the Baptist and withdrew in a boat to a quiet place to be by Himself. But, we are told, 'when the crowds heard it, they followed him on foot from the towns' (verse 13). When Jesus came to the shore, what was His response? Did He get cross and send the crowds away, telling them that this was His 'me time' and to come back later? No. Matthew tells us, 'When he went ashore, he saw a great crowd; and he had compassion for them and cured their sick' (verse 14). He put His 'me time' on hold while He attended to the people, and went back to it later after He had spent time ministering to them, healing them, and feeding more than 5,000 people with five loaves and two fishes!

Jesus needed to recharge His batteries after ministering to the people. If He needed time out, how much more do we need time out?! We desperately need to spend time with our heavenly Father, allowing Him to minister to us, to speak to us and guide us, and to refresh our energies. Yet so often we can use our busyness to avoid spending time with God, or use the time we do spend with Him superficially, because we are afraid that if we allow Him to get too close, He might force us to face something we don't want to face. It might be something from our past that needs dealing with and putting to bed, or it might be an issue that we face currently. It isn't easy to confront these things, but we can be reassured that, far from making us fall apart when we face them, what God actually wants to do is to put us back together again.

I mentioned earlier that I was once involved in a relationship where there was a severe imbalance of power. When I came out of the relationship, I had many issues and fragilities that needed to be dealt with in order for me to move forward. Not that I would admit it. I thought I was fine – I was free, and I figured that because I was now out of the relationship, everything was OK. But if the truth be told, I wasn't OK. My self-esteem was at rock bottom, and I was quite damaged in a number of ways. Yet God had already put people around me to love me and accept me for who I was, and He had already begun to work on me. But I had many fears, one of which was to trust and allow myself to get close to anyone again. I didn't want to put myself in that position again, to give anyone any power over me and to leave open the possibility of being hurt again.

We always think we know best, don't we? But of course, God knows so much better than we do, and knows exactly what we need. I thought I knew what I needed, but God made it very clear that He had other plans for me! He gently led me into another relationship, through which He was able to heal many of my hurts and some of the damage that had been done. I could have carried on as I was and life would have been fine. But because I allowed God, and others, in, and with His help was able to confront some of these issues, He was able to begin to put back together those parts that were broken.

God knows us intimately – even better than we know ourselves – and He knows exactly what we need to make us whole again. We try to hide from Him, and from others, because we don't want to face up to and deal with certain things. We feel comfortable with the familiar, but He wants to set us free from the hold that these things have over us! Issues from our past, and even problems from our present, can hold us back from reaching our true potential. God wants us to face these things so that He can heal us and so that they no longer have any power over us. The healing process may not always be easy, but God is gentle, and He will deal with us in exactly the right way – He knows what we are able to cope with. It *will* be worth it in the long run.

Jesus spent much of His time ministering to the people, but He also made sure He took time out to relax. The Gospels tell us of numerous occasions when Jesus would eat with His friends and followers and enjoy relaxing in their company. In John 12, Jesus was at the home of Lazarus, Mary and Martha. Mary anointed Jesus' feet with some expensive ointment. I am sure this generous act of love would have been a real boost for Jesus. Who among us doesn't like to be ministered to, to be appreciated, in some way or another? Positive experiences where we are made to feel loved and valued give us a boost, mentally, emotionally and even physically.

I have to admit that I struggle with busyness. I work full-time. I have three children, and a house to run. I am also studying part-time and am involved with various ministries in church. It is very easy for me at times to get caught up in the busyness and not take enough time to relax or not spend enough time with the family. But this takes its toll. I get tired very easily, and I have learned the hard way not to push myself too hard or too far – although I confess I still forget at times and think I'm Superwoman! I am aware that I need to stop and take stock of what I am doing on a regular basis, and to be checking regularly that it is still what God wants me to be doing.

It's so easy for us to hide behind this tree of busyness – very often without even realising it! It is important that we stop now and again and take stock of what we are doing, and pray over it all. We need to ask God what it is that *He* wants us to be doing, and step in with His plans, rather than take on too much and wonder why we are unable to cope. I can hear His words now when I say to Him, 'Why am I so tired? Why aren't I coping with all this?'

He says to me, 'Because you didn't ask Me what I wanted you to be doing. You said yes to everything you were asked to do and have become distracted, rather than focusing on what I want you to be doing. Trust Me. I will ensure you have more than enough time and energy to do all the things I want you to do. And I'll make sure you have time for some fun, too!'

Something I have learned over recent years is to use the word 'No' now and again. I find it incredibly hard to do, but it is vital sometimes to our health, our well-being and our sanity! Why do we so often say yes when someone asks us to do something, and ignore that little voice in our head that is saying, 'Don't do it – you know it's too much for you.'

We sometimes say yes because we want to be liked, and we think that by saying yes we are more likely to be accepted and respected. Maybe we know that the person asking is struggling themselves, that they wouldn't ask unless they really needed to, and we really want to do something to help. But then we end up with too much on our own plate. Perhaps subconsciously we feel that the other person is more important than we are in the grand scheme of things, so we feel we ought to be doing what we can to help them.

I can relate to all these reasons. I did them all, and at times I still struggle with them. But we need to remember that it is OK to say no sometimes. People will – or they should – understand if we have a genuine reason for saying no to their request. A relationship built on mutual love and respect can cope with 'No' once in a while. But equally, let's not go too far the other way and fall into the habit of saying no every time. We need to weigh up what we are doing and, if we can, take time to think and pray about what we are committing to before saying yes. It can be so easy to become distracted by things that take our attention away from what God is calling us to do.

Busyness in the church

Busyness can be a particular problem for church leaders. There are many expectations and much pressure put upon them, many of which are totally unrealistic. In a survey by the Evangelical Alliance it was discovered that 68 per cent of church leaders spend more than 40 hours a week on church leadership and ministry activities. Thirty eight per cent said they find it difficult to find time for rest and relaxation, and 25 per cent said that their marriage, family life and friendships suffer because of the demands of ministry. Long working hours and frustrations can also lead to burnout.[2]

The survey also found that 'most people are supportive of and thankful for their church leaders and that most leaders feel privileged and fulfilled'. And there is a 'growing acceptance of shared leadership and recognition that all church members have a role to play'.[3] This is good news! The church is the family of God, the body of Christ, and we have a duty to look after one another – including our leaders. Let us pray for our leaders, and remember that we all have a part to play. God calls us to be a priesthood of believers (see 1 Peter 2:5). The priests were set aside to serve the community. By calling us a 'priesthood' of believers, Peter reminds us that we are called to serve one another.

The church is not a place where a few serve the many; it is for all to serve one another. In this way, the tasks will be shared, and everyone will be looking out for one another, to make sure that they are not overdoing it and risking burnout, whether leaders or 'ordinary' members.

A little bit of R & R

Time to relax and unwind is important. Even God rested on the seventh day of creation. He didn't need to – He is God, after all, and making the world and everything in it would not have tired

Him at all. The Hebrew word for 'rested' in Genesis 2:2 is *shabath*, which means to cease, desist or rest. So it simply means that God stopped working on the seventh day and observed the Sabbath. He also took time out at the end of each previous day to enjoy what He had accomplished that day and to see that it was good. Made as we are in His image, we are to follow His example. We human beings need time to rest from our work. Jesus confirmed this in Mark 2:27 when He said, 'The sabbath was made for humankind, and not humankind for the sabbath.'

Bearing in mind that God created us as relational beings, this seventh day, this time to rest and relax, is a great opportunity to spend time with friends and family, as well as, of course, a chance to recharge our spiritual batteries in fellowship with others.

Time to ourselves is also important. Depending on whether we are extroverts or introverts by nature, we may need to spend time on our own to refresh our energies. Extroverts recharge by spending time with people; introverts need time alone to recharge. Many of us are a bit of both, and need some alone time as well as time with others.

Many people, of course, need to work on Sundays, for various reasons. We need to ensure we take time to rest, and share fellowship with God's people in other ways if we are unable to get to church – perhaps by taking a day off during the week, and attending a house group or another meeting with God's people. The 'one in seven' will look different for different people, but as long as we are stopping and taking the rest and enjoying the fellowship we need, that's OK.

If we find we have too much to do, is there someone to whom we might be able to delegate some of our tasks? For those who are in a supervisory position at work, this might be fairly easy to do – as long as we don't abuse our power and overload our colleagues, of course! More difficult, perhaps, is to delegate jobs within the family, or within the church, or even within social groups. But it is important to recognise when we are taking on too much and to consider whether there is anyone who is better placed – perhaps even someone who is better qualified – and who has more time to do the jobs that otherwise might prove to be too much for us. I appreciate that circumstances for some people make it difficult to do this – for those who are single and have a house to run, for example. There aren't always easy answers, but I believe that somehow God will make a way for us so that we aren't overworked and overtired.

God loves us, and He wants our lives to be satisfying, fulfilling, and fun! God is the inventor of fun, joy and laughter, and He wants us to enjoy our lives! If we ensure we are doing what He wants us to be doing – no less and no more – we can be sure He will meet all our needs.

The fourth 'tree' we sometimes hide behind is the tree of perfectionism – what people think of us. Or perhaps more accurately, what we think people think of us. There is often a wide difference between the two.

Notes

[1] The Living Wage Foundation: http://www.livingwage.org.uk/ (accessed 5th February 2015).
[2] Evangelical Alliance, '21st Century Evangelicals: Life in the church?' Summer 2013, p.19, 23.
[3] 'Life in the church?' p.23.

Chapter 8
The fourth tree: Perfectionism

God saw everything that he had made, and indeed,

it was very good.

Genesis 1:31

Many of us worry about what people think of us – or about what we *think* people think of us. We have a great need to feel that we are good enough, to feel loved and accepted for who we are. As hard as we try, it is impossible to tell ourselves that we are good enough: we need external validation.

But what if who I really am isn't good enough? What if people don't like me for who I am? What if I don't 'look' the part? So we try to change the way we look, or the way we speak, or the way we behave, because we need to feel that we 'fit'. How many times have you looked in astonishment as a friend of yours answered the phone to their boss or to a colleague, or to someone else they were anxious to impress, using a voice that was totally different from the voice they use in conversation with you? I'm aware that I do it – I have a 'telephone voice' that I use when I speak to clients, which is not the same as the voice I would use when I'm speaking to a friend or family member! We change things about ourselves in order to project a particular image because we are anxious to impress or to fit in.

We spend much energy trying to make ourselves who we think people want us to be, and trying to change ourselves according to what we believe people think of us. But our perception of what people think of us is often wrong. So we spend all this time and energy trying to make something different of ourselves, when actually the person we are underneath is the person people really want to get to know. We try to hide who we really are by being something different. The danger is that we can end up pushing people away because they realise that the person we are trying to project isn't the real person inside. It's ironic that in trying to be someone who will be accepted by others, we can end up being rejected because we come across as false and insincere.

This is something I struggled with for many years. Because I didn't feel that I was particularly loveable, I thought that people wouldn't like me if I allowed the real me to come to the surface. So I kept myself to myself and didn't let people in. The 'me' I put on show was someone who I thought people would want to be with, yet deep inside I knew it wasn't working, so I withdrew even more.

It was only when God very gently pointed this out to me that I began to realise what I was doing. By His grace, and with the help of some very loving and patient people He put around me, I very gradually felt able to allow the real me to come to the surface. Amazingly, I discovered that people actually liked me! What a shock!

I learned that what people really want is authenticity, not perfection. I began to understand that it was OK to make mistakes – that people wouldn't reject me because I had got something wrong or said something daft. I learned to relax more with people, and to just be me.

Don't get me wrong – I still have a long way to go. I still tie myself up in knots at times for the silliest things, and worry about what people might think, but I am learning to go with WYSIWYG (what you see is what you get). This is me, warts and all, like it or not. Perhaps that sounds a bit harsh – as if I've gone too far the other way. I haven't – it just means I make an effort not to get worked up worrying about what people think about me and the things I do. I'm learning that people are actually way more accepting of me if I allow myself to be truly myself and stop worrying about it, than if I am completely stressed trying to be someone that I'm not. I am taking on board that God is the only one I need to please – He is the one I am answerable to. If I make it my priority to do what pleases Him, the rest will fall into its natural and rightful place.

Media madness

One of the things we worry about most is the way we look. How many of us felt like we were the dowdy one in our friendship group at school? Me! I had a friend at school who was physically very attractive, with olive skin, dark hair and dark eyes – and never a zit in sight! She also had a really lovely, bubbly personality, she was bright and always achieved good marks, she was funny and witty, and everyone liked her. I felt like the 'also-ran', the dull, plain-looking friend. Not that she made me feel like that – it was likely as not all in my head.

In my opinion, the media has much to answer for here. We want to live up to the images we see portrayed in magazines, on billboards and on the television. We want to look like the beautiful people we see in the media, and we spend time and much money on products, procedures and even surgery to improve the way we look.

Yet these images are not real. Many – if not the majority – are digitally altered to enhance the final images that we see on the pages or on our screens. Wrinkles and blemishes are ironed out, skin tone is enriched, breasts are enlarged, legs are lengthened and waistlines are reduced. If you do an internet search for 'photoshopped images', you will come across many 'before and after' pictures of celebrities and others.

Lady Gaga famously criticised a photograph of her that appeared on the front cover of a glamour magazine, saying that it is not what she looks like when she wakes up in the morning. 'I felt my skin looked too perfect,' she said. 'I felt my hair looked too soft.'[1] In effect, what she was really saying was, 'That's not me. That's not who I am.'

We can try so hard to live up to what we are told is 'normal', but in fact we are striving after the impossible. The images presented to us are effectually the product of someone's imagination. A while ago I came across a short video clip that shows very clearly how different a person can be made to look. You see the woman being photographed and what she looks like in real life, the photoshopping process, and then the final image. It's quite staggering.[2] I wonder how she might have felt at the end of the process. She is an attractive woman, but how must she have felt to see the way her looks had been 'improved'? Would it have had an effect on her self-image? I very much doubt whether my self-confidence would be robust enough to undergo such a process.

I find it quite frightening that this fixation with our looks starts in childhood – even with the toys we play with. Many of us will have played with Barbie dolls as children, and many of our children still do today. More than a billion Barbie dolls have been sold since her 'birth' in 1959. Yet Barbie's looks are not true to life. Research has shown that if she were to be scaled up to human size, her proportions would be similar to those of an anorexic. Her pro-rata measurements would be 36–18–33. How unrealistic are those?! Her neck would be so thin it would barely be able to support the weight of her head.

Nickolay Lamm created a mock-up of Barbie using the measurements of an average 19-year-old woman. The result was a doll that looked very different to the Barbie that is now so familiar to us.[3] He has a vision to create a family of dolls, called Lammily dolls. He says, 'The foundation of Lammily is built on being true to yourself in a world that pressures you to conform to standards.' And he adds, 'Lammily's wardrobe will be realistic as well.'[4]

We need to be very careful not to get sucked in to the feeling that we are not good enough as we are. And we need to make sure our children don't get sucked in either. It's so easy to be caught out, and to end up in a downward spiral that can lead to all sorts of problems, including eating disorders. A recent report states that the number of 13- to 19-year-olds admitted to hospital with eating disorders has increased 89 per cent in three years and has almost tripled since 2003–04. The majority of these cases were female, and the average age was 15. In reality, the numbers could be higher, as many sufferers don't go to hospital. The report acknowledges that images in the media of 'perfect looking' people is putting teenagers under a lot of pressure, leading to body image dissatisfaction and low self-esteem.[5]

Good enough is good enough

Perfectionism also expresses itself in what we do. We may feel that unless we achieve good grades in our exams, or hit high targets in our work, or produce work that is error free, what we produce will not be good enough. I have battled with this for many years, and I still struggle sometimes to accept that 'good enough' can be good enough. I guess my work as an editor and proofreader means I am always looking to correct errors and to present a perfect manuscript. But there are many other areas of my life where I don't have to deliver perfection. Of course, in an ideal world, everything we do would be perfectly produced, but that is not the reality of the society in which we live. We need to discern when perfection is appropriate, and when it is really not necessary. Sometimes the effort required by perfection is totally disproportionate to the purpose and impact of the finished result.

I am on a journey to understanding that I will still be loved and accepted – by God and by my family and friends – even though I make mistakes. I am also learning to laugh at my mistakes, when appropriate!

What about Jesus?

Jesus was the embodiment of God on earth, the Son of God, and by His very nature He was perfect. So we will not find in the Gospels any examples of Jesus accepting Himself in spite of His shortcomings – because He didn't have any! What we can do, though, is find numerous examples of Jesus' love for and acceptance of other people in spite of their limitations and weaknesses.

Every person who came to Jesus in true humility was totally accepted by Him. He said Himself that He had 'come to call not the righteous but sinners' (Mark 2:17). Jesus went to eat with Levi, the tax collector, even though this raised many an eyebrow. Mark tells us:

> And as he sat at dinner in Levi's house, many tax-collectors and sinners were also sitting with Jesus and his disciples – for there were many who followed him. When the scribes of the Pharisees saw that he was eating with sinners and tax-collectors, they said to his disciples, 'Why does he eat with tax-collectors and sinners?'
> *Mark 2:15-16*

Jesus didn't just 'put up' with sinners, tolerating them because He had no choice; He welcomed them, He ate with them, and He made a deliberate choice to spend His time with them.

When Jesus began His ministry, He didn't go to the temples and synagogues to seek out followers from among the 'holy' people. He looked for ordinary people who were living ordinary lives and doing ordinary jobs. He also sought out those with big difficulties and troubles, such as 'Legion', the man with many demons (Luke 8:26-33), and Mary Magdalene, who had been released from 'seven demons', among other women 'who had been cured of evil spirits and infirmities' (Luke 8:2).

As people spent time with Jesus, they often became aware of their own shortcomings – and Jesus never stopped loving them. Peter became acutely aware of Jesus' holiness after the miraculous catch of fish, and he said to Jesus, 'Go away from me, Lord, for I am a sinful man!'

What was Jesus response? 'Do not be afraid…' (Luke 5:8-10).

How often, when we become aware of the shortcomings of others, are we tempted to be judgemental and critical? I am humbled when I look at the response of Jesus. Not only does He tell Peter not to be afraid, but He also gives him a job to do: He tells him that from now on he will be 'catching people'. God doesn't wait until we achieve perfection before He is able to use us for kingdom purposes. He takes us as we are, warts and all, blesses us and gives us a job to do. Each one of us. There is not a single person on earth who is not good enough for God to use.

God created us in His image and according to His likeness, and He deliberately created us all to be different. We are different shapes and sizes. We are different colours, with different colour hair and eyes. We have different features and different personalities. God did this by design; it wasn't an accident. And you were not an accident either! God designed you carefully and lovingly, in His image, exactly how He wanted you to be!

We should embrace and enjoy our differences. We should enjoy being the person God created us to be, rather than wishing we were more like somebody else. We are all works in progress, yes, but God will always equip us to do what He wants us to do. My journey will be different from your journey. God will equip me for my journey, and He will equip you for your journey, and what He equips me with will of course be different from what He equips you with. If I try to be like you instead of embracing who God has created me to be, I will struggle on my journey, because my equipping will not match the tasks I am endeavouring to carry out. But if I embrace who I am and take hold of what God has given me, I will find satisfaction and fulfilment as I am able to use the unique mix of gifts I have been given to meet the opportunities and challenges I will come across along my road.

God invites us to take His hand and step out from behind the tree of perfectionism, and to drop the fig leaf of the need for faultlessness in everything we do. Let us accept ourselves for who we are, while acknowledging that God still has work to do in us. God is gracious, and He is able to use us in spite of our limitations and shortcomings. Indeed, often He chooses to work through them. We only have to look at some of the heroes of the Bible to see that not a single one was without fault. Moses committed murder. David committed adultery and murder. Abraham lied and said that his wife was his sister. Peter denied Jesus three times at the most crucial moment of His life. Saul (before he became the apostle Paul) was a persecutor and killer of Christians. Yet these people, and many more, are the backbone of our faith, and God used them to do amazing things for Him.

No matter what we have done or how much of a failure we think we are, God loves us and accepts us. We don't have to live up to the standards the media sets – it's not as if they are achievable anyway. Neither do we have to try to be like anyone else. Just be who you are. Trust me – it's liberating!

The fifth 'tree' we will look at is the tree of pretence, of what we choose to believe.

Notes

[1] Margot Peppers, '"I do not look like this when I wake up": Lady Gaga criticizes her own Glamour cover for making her appear "too perfect"', *Mail Online*, 13th November 2013. Available at http://www.dailymail.co.uk/femail/article-2506274/Lady-Gaga-criticizes-Glamour-cover-perfect.html (accessed 11th July 2014).

[2] Laura Willard, 'See why we have an absolutely ridiculous standard of beauty in just 37 seconds', *Upworthy*. Available at http://www.upworthy.com/see-why-we-have-an-absolutely-ridiculous-standard-of-beauty-in-just-37-seconds (accessed 11th July 2014).

[3] Nikolay Lamm, 'What would Barbie look like as an average woman?' 22nd December 2013. Available at http://nickolaylamm.com/art-for-clients/what-would-barbie-look-like-as-an-average-woman/ (accessed 11th July 2014).

[4] Nikolay Lamm, 'The future of Lammily', 13th April 2014. Available at http://nickolaylamm.com/ (accessed 14th July 2014).

[5] Carey Lodge, 'Teen hospital admissions for eating disorders nearly double in three years', *Christian Today*, 3rd June 2015. Available at http://www.christiantoday.com/article/teen.hospital.admissions.for.eating.disorders.nearly.doubles.in.three.years/55311.htm (accessed 11th June 2015).

Chapter 9
The fifth tree: Pretence

Jesus said to him, 'Have you believed because
you have seen me? Blessed are those who have
not seen and yet have come to believe.'

John 20:29

Did you know that the six moon landings documented between 1969 and 1972 didn't really happen? They were fabricated by NASA so that they wouldn't lose their funding. Did you also know that Elvis Presley didn't really die in 1977? His death was faked and he was put into a witness protection scheme as a drug informant. And did you know that many of today's world leaders are actually alien reptilian humanoids who must consume human blood to maintain their human appearance?

These are just a few of the weird and wacky conspiracy theories that some people believe. We may chuckle at some of the things people choose to believe, and we probably find it hard to understand quite how and why they should consider that these things might even be possible. Yet the fact is that some people really do believe them.

What is it that makes us decide what we want to believe? How do we choose what we will judge to be true?

In today's Western society where we are heavily reliant on technology, reality is becoming more and more relative. If we don't like something, we can switch it off, or switch over, or hide our head in the sand and pretend it isn't happening. There are so many sad and depressing stories in the news, so perhaps it isn't surprising that sometimes we feel we cannot take any more bad news and choose not to listen, or elect to listen to something that lightens our hearts instead.

We live in a world where information is constantly at our fingertips. We have the internet at our disposal whenever we need or want it, and news is available 24/7, on countless television channels, radio stations, websites and mobile apps. Whereas once we could 'escape' when we were out of the house, it is more difficult even to do that now, as it is always with us on our smartphones or tablets or on the car radio. It's information overload. But by its very nature, this vast amount of information means there is always an alternative, so if we don't like the particular spin that is used by one channel or website, we can switch to another that is more sympathetic to our beliefs. Or we can switch everything off and choose to hear nothing at all.

We can find evidence to back up almost any viewpoint we hold, no matter how strange or way-out that belief might be. Conspiracy theories abound, and for those whose imaginations enjoy running riot, there will always be people who are willing to listen and believe!

I have to confess that I can be quite gullible at times. I guess it is because I like to believe the best of people, and I usually choose to believe that they are being genuine rather than that they would tell me untruths. Having said that, though, if someone does lie to me, it takes a long time to restore my trust. I watch body language to try to discern whether or not people are telling me the truth. I'm no expert, and I often get it wrong, but sometimes I can get a 'feel' for people if I listen to what my gut is telling me.

Lies are very damaging. This was something Abraham discovered, when many people suffered as a result of a lie he told. He and his family went to Egypt because there was a famine in the land where they were living. Sarai, his wife, was very beautiful, and he was worried that he would be killed and they would let her live. So he instructed her to say that she was his sister. Consequently, Sarai was taken into Pharaoh's house, and

Pharaoh gave to Abram (as he was still known at that time) many livestock and servants.

But we are told that 'the Lord afflicted Pharaoh and his house with great plagues because of Sarai, Abram's wife'. Pharaoh realised that Sarai was Abram's wife and was angry with Abram for lying to him, and sent them away (Genesis 12:10-20). I'm guessing that it was only Pharaoh's fear of what else God might do to him if he were to kill Abram that saved Abram and Sarai's lives.

It is very tempting to take matters into our own hands and not to trust God, but God had great plans for Abraham and Sarah, and there is no doubt He would have protected them if they were to have told the truth. This is easy for us to see, with the benefit of knowing the bigger picture, but a lot harder to do when we feel that we or our loved ones could be in danger.

Many relationships are destroyed because of lies. How can we trust someone who has a known track record of lying? It only takes a single lie to destroy trust, and when trust is lost, one of the basic foundations of a relationship is destroyed, and it takes a long time to rebuild it – if indeed it can ever be rebuilt. This is why it is so important to be truthful, and to be known as a truthful person.

It is also why it is so important that we keep our promises. If we are unsure whether we will be able to keep a promise, surely it is better not to make it in the first place. This is something I have always tried to do, particularly with my children. When we are making plans, if there is a chance that something might happen to get in the way of those plans, I will tell them that we hope to be able to do it, or that we will do it if this or that happens. That way, when I do make them a promise, they know I will keep it. Children need to be able to trust others, in the same way as they need to learn the importance of being trustworthy themselves and of always telling the truth.

Trust is a foundation stone of all relationships, and as relational beings made in the image of God, we cannot afford to overlook it. Without the foundation of trust, the house will crumble and fall.

Mind games

Does your mind ever play tricks on you? How many times have you left the house and then wondered whether you locked the front door properly, or whether you closed the bedroom window? This is something I do regularly! I was a single parent for a few years when my children were younger, and every night I would check all the doors and windows downstairs before going upstairs to bed. But then I would lie in bed and wonder whether I had locked them all properly. I would remind myself that I had checked them all and they were definitely all locked, but I just could not relax and go to sleep until I went downstairs to check them all over again! Never once did I find that any were unlocked! Now at least there are two of us to check them all before we go to bed!

When we go away on holiday, my family know what I am like, and they will always reassure me when I question halfway through our journey that the front door is properly locked. On one occasion, my son even took a video recording on his phone so he could show me later when I asked the question!

Our minds are able to convince us of things that are not really the truth. They play games with us, particularly during the night-time hours. The hours of darkness are the times when we tend to worry the most. During the daytime our attention is occupied with many other things, so we do not dwell on things – or, at least, we dwell on them less – but at night, when we are relaxed, our minds are bombarded with all sorts of ideas and thoughts. We need to discern which are good thoughts and which are bad thoughts, and consciously reject the bad ones.

I find I worry more at night, probably because my mind has more time to think and to wander. I find myself imagining all sorts of dreadful scenarios, particularly if one of the children is out late, and then I have trouble sleeping. Why don't I have thoughts like these during the daytime? Perhaps because my mind is more occupied, or perhaps the darkness throws a whole different perspective on things. I know I need to switch off and try to tell myself that it is just my imagination, and that the odds of this particular scenario happening are remote, but once my mind starts wandering down that road, it can be difficult to bring it back.

I guess my mind is more open to suggestion at night, perhaps because I am more relaxed, or simply because I'm not filling my head with work, family matters, and everything else I find myself doing and thinking about during the daytime. Sometimes God speaks to me – again, probably because it is one of the few times He can actually get through to me, but I am aware of the need to discern whether it is His voice speaking to me or whether it is my imagination going for a walk again.

As I say, God sometimes speaks to me at night, either just after I have gone to bed and before I go to sleep, or if I wake up during the night. Occasionally He will speak to me through a dream. For many years I have kept a notebook by the side of the bed so I can scribble down any thoughts I have, so that I can be sure to remember them the next day. Sometimes it will be something entirely mundane, such as remembering to add something to the shopping list, but at other times it might be something more profound. The only problem I have in the morning is deciphering the scrawl I have written in the dark! On a number of occasions I have got up to write an article, a talk or a chapter of a book, because inspiration has taken hold of me and my mind is buzzing with ideas. While this is perhaps a little frustrating (especially for someone who needs and enjoys their sleep as much as I do), it is also a joy. I am learning to discern the voice of God in the hours of darkness, and to respond when I believe He is speaking.

Do you ever have trouble sleeping? If so, next time it happens, consider the possibility that God is knocking on your window, trying to attract your attention. Perhaps He has something specific He wants to say to you, or perhaps He just wants to spend some time with you, to enjoy your company for a while. Open the door and let Him in, and sit together for a while. Relax with Him, curl up in His arms, let Him stroke your hair, and hear Him tell you how much He loves you. You are His son, His daughter, and He longs to enjoy and deepen His relationship with you.

What about Jesus?

Jesus was absolutely sure of His beliefs. He knew who He was, He knew His Father, and He knew what He had come to earth to do. There was no doubt in His mind, and He would not be swayed from His beliefs or His purpose.

In Luke's Gospel we are told that early in His ministry, Jesus went to the synagogue in Nazareth and stood up to read from the scroll of the prophet Isaiah. He read from Isaiah 61:

> '"The Spirit of the Lord is upon me,
> because he has anointed me
> to bring good news to the poor.
> He has sent me to proclaim release to the captives
> and recovery of sight to the blind,
> to let the oppressed go free,
> to proclaim the year of the Lord's favour."
> ... Today this scripture has been fulfilled in your hearing.'
> *Luke 4:18-19, 21*

Jesus was very sure of Himself, and of the job He had come to do. He spoke these words even though He knew He would be rejected by the people in His home town. And indeed, just a few short verses later, we are told that:

> When they heard this, all in the synagogue were filled with rage. They got up, drove him out of the town, and led him to the brow of the hill on which their town was built, so that they might hurl him off the cliff.
> *Luke 4:28-29*

Surely this would have been a terrifying experience! I can only imagine how I might respond if people were to try to throw me off a cliff. But did Jesus panic? Did He back down? Did He regret what He had said and try to take back His words because He had offended some people? No – He simply walked through the crowd and went on His way (Luke 4:30).

Such certainty in His belief. Such confidence in God His Father. How did He do it?

Well, partly because of the amount of time Jesus spent in prayer. We have covered this already in chapter 3, so I won't go into it again here. But suffice it to say that as He spent time with God, Jesus was being strengthened. It is likely He was also receiving His instructions and learning what the Father wanted Him to do. Perhaps He was receiving words of knowledge about people He would meet, or God would tell Him where He was to go next to minister.

We, too, need to make sure we spend time with God. By spending time with our heavenly Father we learn what He wants for us, and we begin to adopt His characteristics and start to 'look' more like Him, as we draw closer to His image and likeness. We are influenced by those we spend the most time with. The more time we spend with God, the more we become like Him, and the more we get to know what His purposes are for our lives. Then we will have the strength to stand firm when we are questioned, and even when we suffer because of our beliefs.

We sometimes find it hard to believe that God would allow bad things to happen. If He is a God of love, why is there such suffering in the world? As I talk sometimes to non-Christians, I find that this is overwhelmingly the question they ask. I certainly don't know all the answers, but I do believe that the suffering that exists in the world today is a direct consequence of the Fall of humankind. We saw in chapter 3 that the immediate consequences of Adam and Eve's sin were that they had to leave God's beautiful garden and that humanity's physical, spiritual and relational resemblance to God was severely damaged and distorted. Death, sickness and decay became a part of humanity's reality; looking after the earth became hard work; the balance of the relationship between men and women was upset; there would be pain in childbirth and there would be enmity between the humans and the serpent (Genesis 3:15). The natural order and balance of the world had been upset, and the relationship between humankind and the rest of creation had been damaged.

If Christians were to be somehow protected from suffering because of our relationship with God, wouldn't everyone become Christians just so they could have this immunity? I don't believe that is the kind of relationship God wants to have with us. It isn't an insurance policy, nor is it about buying a ticket to heaven. God has given us free will, and He wants us to love Him and have a relationship with Him because we want to and because we love Him; not because of what we can get out of it.

Suffering by definition is never easy, but I believe we can find three positive things that can come out of it.

Firstly, God loves all people equally, and He doesn't show favouritism. Suffering happens because it is a consequence of the evil that has entered the world. God doesn't give us immunity from it, but He does equip us to cope. I can look back on particular experiences in my own life and see how God clearly put people around me to help me cope with the difficult times that He knew were coming. As I look back, I can clearly see His hand on the whole situation, and although He didn't prevent the difficulties happening, He did equip me and stay close to me and give me the strength I needed to get through them.

One of the most difficult times I have ever faced was going through a marriage break-up and divorce. To be truly honest, the relationship had died years before and I had done pretty much all of my grieving for it before the separation. The hardest part was helping my children through the situation. But God put people around us to love us and support us, people who were there for us, day and night, people who would listen when we needed to talk, offer practical help when we needed it, and just love us without judging us or our circumstances.

Secondly, God is able to use the experiences we have been through to bless and help others who are going through similar situations. While I do not believe God ever plans and designs suffering for us, I know He is the Redeemer, and somehow He is able to turn around even the most difficult and tragic situations and use them for good, if we are willing to allow Him to. As I have shared some of my experiences with others, whether through my first book, through speaking engagements or through one-to-one chats with people, I have been humbled by the number of people who have told me they are able to relate to what I say and have been helped and encouraged by it. I find that people will talk to me about their own experiences because they know I understand. We all like to talk to people who really 'get it', who understand what we are saying and can relate to what we are going through. I don't have the answers to their difficulties. Sometimes I may be able to offer a few words that might help, but often people just want to talk and unload, and it is a privilege that they choose me to do that with.

The third way God can use our suffering is to help us to appreciate what we have! My husband and I have both been through difficult relationships and have been married before. While we would never have chosen to go through some of the things we went through, there are some things that we would not change in a million years – the seven children and three grandchildren we have between us, for one thing! And because we know where we have come from, it makes us really appreciate what God has given us in one another. God has also used us both to bring healing to one another – healing of old hurts and wounds, some of which we didn't even realise were there. And as we share our story with others, we hope and pray that it will bring hope and encouragement to them, too.

The witness of the martyrs

As Christians, it is important for us to be aware of what is going on in the world, and it is important that we choose wisely our sources of information. We are called to be alert and to be on watch, so that we can pray. One of the biggest issues facing Christians in many countries of the world today is persecution.

Throughout the history of the Christian church, followers of Jesus have suffered for what they believe, and many have been martyred for their faith. It continues to happen today in many countries across the world. I understand that more Christians were martyred for their faith in the twentieth century than in the previous 19 centuries put together, so the situation is getting worse. More than 26 million cases of Christian martyrs were documented in the twentieth century, compared with 14 million between AD 33 and 1900.[1] As I write, there are terrible accounts all over the news of the persecution and execution of Christians in the Middle East.

Yet this should not surprise us. Jesus gave clear warnings that His followers would face persecution:

> 'They will arrest you and persecute you; they will hand you over to synagogues and prisons, and you will be brought before kings and governors because of my name ... You will be betrayed even by parents and brothers, by relatives and friends; and they will put some of you to death. You will be hated by all because of my name. But not a hair of your head will perish. By your endurance you will gain your souls.'
> *Luke 21:12, 16-19*

He also said, 'If they persecuted me, they will persecute you' (John 15:20). And, of course, they did persecute Jesus, all the way to His execution on a cross.

So, as Christians, we are not immune to persecution. But let's look a little deeper and go back to Luke 21, where Jesus also says:

> 'This will give you an opportunity to testify. So make up your minds not to prepare your defence in advance; for I will give you words and a wisdom that none of your opponents will be able to withstand or contradict.'
> *Luke 21:13-15*

And in Matthew's Gospel He says:

> 'Blessed are those who are persecuted for righteousness' sake, for theirs is the kingdom of heaven.
>
> 'Blessed are you when people revile you and persecute you and utter all kinds of evil against you falsely on my account. Rejoice and be glad, for your reward is great in heaven, for in the same way they persecuted the prophets who were before you.'
> *Matthew 5:10-12*

So there *will* be persecution – that, unfortunately, is inevitable. The majority of us in the West are very blessed to enjoy religious freedom, and we are unlikely to ever experience the level of torture and suffering for our faith that many in other countries do. But we might still be on the receiving end of criticism and mocking for our beliefs. Although not on the scale that some experience, this can still be hurtful, but we can pray that God will show us how we can use these occasions as opportunities to witness to our faith. Jesus says that the Holy Spirit will show us what to say. He won't leave us to handle it alone. Plus, there is a great reward waiting in heaven!

Now I'm certainly not suggesting that we should welcome or invite persecution! No one wants to experience such awful suffering, and my heart goes out to all who are undergoing such dreadful torture. But God equips and strengthens His children when they need it most. The very first martyr, Stephen, about whom we are told in chapter 7 of Acts, is a great example of this:

> When they heard these things, they became enraged and ground their teeth at Stephen. But filled with the Holy Spirit, he gazed into heaven and saw the glory of God and Jesus standing at the right hand of God. 'Look,' he said, 'I see the heavens opened and the Son of Man standing at the right hand of God!'
> Acts 7:54-56

Stephen was stoned to death for his beliefs, yet at the point of his greatest suffering, he had a vision of Jesus standing at the right hand of God, waiting to welcome him home!

The rest of the New Testament contains many accounts of persecution of the first followers of Jesus: they were thrown into prison, stoned, flogged and scoffed at, and many were killed for believing in Him. Yet God used them to bear witness and to spread the good news of Jesus, and the early church grew at a rate that has rarely been seen since. Paul even rejoiced in his sufferings, viewing them as opportunities to share in the suffering that Christ had endured, and he considered it a privilege to suffer for his Lord:

> So, I will boast all the more gladly of my weaknesses, so that the power of Christ may dwell in me. Therefore I am content with weaknesses, insults, hardships, persecutions, and calamities for the sake of Christ; for whenever I am weak, then I am strong.
> *2 Corinthians 12:9-10*

> For he has graciously granted you the privilege not only of believing in Christ, but of suffering for him as well.
> *Philippians 1:29*

And he endured his suffering for the benefit of his fellow followers:

> I pray therefore that you may not lose heart over my sufferings for you; they are your glory.
> *Ephesians 3:13*

As I have just mentioned, during the early years of Christianity, the church was growing at a rapid rate. How could this be, when Christians were being killed for their faith?! Wouldn't people be deterred from believing something and joining a movement that might well get them killed? That was what the authorities thought, which was why they continued to persecute the Christians, but it actually had the opposite effect. It was as a direct result of some of these persecutions that many people came to faith in Christ. They witnessed the faith and the courage of the martyrs, and considered that there had to be something in this Christianity business for them not only to be prepared to die for their beliefs, but also to be so calm and courageous in the face of such pain and brutality.

Justin Martyr was one such person. In the second century he witnessed the brutal execution of a number of Christians in Rome and was very moved by their courage and serenity. He became a Christian himself, and was later martyred for his faith. He said:

> We do not give up our confession though we be executed by the sword, though we be crucified, thrown to wild beasts, put in chains, and exposed to fire and every other kind of torture. Everyone knows this. On the contrary, the more we are persecuted and martyred, the more do others in ever increasing numbers become believers and God-fearing people through the name of Jesus.[2]

How do we react in the face of our own suffering, when we are mocked for our beliefs? Do we endure patiently, lovingly and courageously, or do we just complain that life isn't fair? How much more of a witness to Jesus would we be if we were to trust Him to guide us and to fill our mouths with His words, as He promised, instead of taking the opportunity to complain about our lot in life?

Persecution, tragically, will continue, and I am sure God will continue to use it to bear witness to the good news. But that doesn't make it right, and it doesn't make it acceptable. We must pray for our brothers and sisters who are being killed, persecuted and imprisoned for their faith. Let us pray that God will sustain and strengthen them, and set them free. It is equally important that we pray for those who are persecuting them, that their eyes will be opened and that they will see and know the truth about Jesus. Let us pray that the image of God in human beings will enable all people to embrace diversity and to seek understanding where there are differences of opinion, with love and respect for one another.

Standing firm

So what do we believe? Who do we believe? Do we cherry-pick what we listen to on the news, what we read on the internet and in the newspapers, to make it more palatable? I confess that I'm guilty of this at times. It can be hard to cope when we see so much suffering, day in, day out, yet those who are living in these conditions have no choice but to face them every day of their lives. There is no let-up. Our hearts can become hardened to the suffering of others because we feel we are faced with it constantly, and it ceases to affect us. We, though, can switch off the television or the radio, or turn the page of the newspaper. There is no 'off' switch for them.

We often choose what we want to believe because it makes life easier for us. We hide behind these beliefs because they fit comfortably with our worldview. But sometimes we need to face the hard questions and wrestle with them. I confess that there are things in the Bible that I don't understand. There are things about the Christian life that I don't understand. Perhaps I will never understand them this side of heaven. But my overriding belief is that God is a God of love, and that He wants good things for His children and for His creation. I choose to believe that the bad things that are in this world do not come from God, but He allows them to happen, partly because they are consequences of the sin of humankind, and partly because He is able to turn them around and use them for good. I accept that there are things I do not understand, and I trust in God's wisdom. He, after all, can see the whole picture; I can only see a small part of it.

When we face difficult times, what is our anchor? Do we endeavour to draw our strength from ourselves and our own resources, or do we turn to God and His word, to prayer and to the community God has put around us to strengthen us and help us through? Are we grounded in His word, so that when we are challenged about what we believe we are able to give an answer and explain why we hold such an opinion? Where do we look for answers to some of life's difficult questions? The Bible, or Google?

What we believe determines how we live, how we act and how we react in particular situations. Our beliefs, once they become ingrained in our minds and hearts, even feed into our instincts. Our minds are fed by what we read, hear, watch and absorb from what is going on around us, from our friends, our colleagues, the culture in which we live, and so on. It is much easier to go with the flow than to stand up and be counted, to be different. We each have to decide for ourselves how we will live, what we choose to believe and the standards by which we will live. When that looks different to the way those around us choose to live, it can be hard. How do we find the courage to stand up and be counted, to do the right thing, even when it looks as though we might be the only one?

Jesus wasn't afraid to be different. He wasn't put off by what people thought. He was so deeply rooted in God His Father, in Scripture, that He knew in every situation the right thing to do. He knew where His identity lay – in His relationship with God His Father – and He wasn't afraid to be different. His knowledge of God's word was so much a part of Him that He was able to take on the teachers of the Law and challenge the interpretations that had been followed for centuries. I am aware that my own knowledge of Scripture is weak, and I pray that God will help me as I read His word to enable me to ingest it so that it becomes a part of who I am, and that my beliefs and values will be the ones He would have me hold on to.

The martyrs, both then and now, could have chosen to believe something different, to deny Jesus and to worship another. This would make life very much easier for them. But they choose to continue to believe in the teachings of Jesus and to follow Him, no matter what the cost. Would I be prepared to do the same? Would you?

How do we spend our free time? Let's have a look now at the sixth and final tree: the tree of pastimes.

Notes

[1] Dan Wooding, 'Modern persecution', Church history timeline 1901–2000. Available at http://www.christianity.com/church/church-history/timeline/1901-2000/modern-persecution-11630665.html (accessed 7th May 2015).
[2] Justin Martyr, cited in Gerald L. Sittser, *Water from a deep well: Christian spirituality from early martyrs to modern missionaries* (Downers Grove: IVP, 2007), p.33.

Chapter 10
The sixth tree: Pastimes

Finally, beloved, whatever is true, whatever is
honourable, whatever is just, whatever is pure,
whatever is pleasing, whatever is commendable, if
there is any excellence and if there is anything
worthy of praise, think about these things.

Philippians 4:8

We all have ways we like to escape for a while. Some like to read a good novel; others lose themselves in craft activities; some enjoy watching films or television, listening to music or doing puzzles; others like to play games or participate in sport. Whatever we choose to do, we all need some form of diversion. Life can be hard, and a little bit of escapism now and again is perfectly healthy – and necessary.

I love to read. There are few things I enjoy more than losing myself in a good book. These days, though, I don't get much time to read for pleasure. I read for a living, and with the reading I need to do for my studies as well, often the last thing I want to do in my spare time is pick up a book! When I go on holiday, though, I really look forward to the opportunity to get stuck into a good read. My only problem then is how to choose between all the things on my list that I want to read!

When you have a free hour or so, how do you choose to spend it? Do you read a book, watch a film, play sport, play computer or console games, while it away on a social network? Would you have a coffee with a friend? Or perhaps you might catch up on some sleep! Whatever we do, it's very important that we all take time out deliberately to relax and unwind.

Making room for creativity

I have tremendous admiration for anyone who can draw, paint, sculpt or do anything that is what I would call visually artistic. I can barely draw a stick person, and don't consider myself to be artistic in that way at all. For many years, in fact, I didn't consider myself to be at all creative, yet in recent years I have been discovering creativity in myself in the form of writing. Creativity is an important way of expressing ourselves, and we all have this ability within us in some form or another. It might take the form of drawing or painting, making music, writing, fashion, interior design, cooking, or in the way we decorate our home or in the clothes we wear.

For many years I didn't have the confidence to make choices in decorating my home. I didn't think I had wisdom or good enough taste when it came to choices of colours and accessories. But then my hallway was in desperate need of a makeover. So I chose the colours I wanted and arranged for it to be done. I was thrilled with the result, and had a number of comments about how nice it looked. This really boosted my confidence, and when my husband and I got married and wanted to give our living room a much-needed facelift, I had much more confidence in making suggestions and choices.

I realise our taste and our creativity may not be everybody's cup of tea, but our home now (or, at least, the rooms we have been able to work on) is an expression of who we are. Taste is just that – our own personal taste, and it is different for everyone. My taste will be different to the next person's, but that is part of the beauty of the world, and to enjoy and appreciate those differences is a great gift.

'Everything in moderation'

This is one of the things my mother used to say to me when I was growing up. If I remember rightly, she was referring to food and the need for a balanced diet, and saying that the odd treat here and there would do us no harm.

This, though, is a good principle to apply to the whole of our lives. We can spend too much time and energy on one or two things, to the detriment of the others, leading to imbalance, burnout and focus on all sorts of unhealthy stuff, if things are allowed to get out of hand.

There is another saying I'm sure we have all heard: 'You are what you eat.' I have heard a number of variations of this, such as, 'You are what you think about.' Physically, our bodies reflect what we eat. And what we think about is reflected in our words, our actions and our attitudes. This is why we need to be careful how we spend our free time. It is good – indeed, vital – that we relax, but everything we do feeds our mind and our character. Many of the pastimes we choose can be healthy and good for us, and I am sure I don't need to say that the opposite can also be true. There are many things vying for our attention (and for our money), some of which might even be dangerous and lead to addiction or other unwholesome behaviour and attitudes.

I am often concerned when I see some of what is presented on television, particularly what is targeted at children and young people. On more than one occasion as my children were growing up I stopped them watching particular programmes because I felt they were not portraying healthy relationships and attitudes. It is so easy to watch things on television and to think that what we are seeing is the norm, when the reality is drastically different. This colours our view of the world, which can end up severely distorted, whether because of the fictional programmes we watch, or because of bias in the reporting of events on the news.

Focusing our minds and our attention too much on things that are not good for us is likely to have a detrimental effect on our relationships, not least our relationship with God. 'I can handle it,' we say with confidence, but before we know it we find ourselves at the bottom of a slippery slope.

It is important that we stop and take stock every now and again of what we are doing and why. If our use of our spare time is having a negative effect on some other areas in our lives, maybe it is time to rethink and find other ways to relax and unwind.

High-tech hobbies

In today's technological age, there are numerous ways of spending our free time that were not available when I was growing up. Today's younger generation has embraced this 'new' technology and made it their own. But they are not alone. Indeed, I myself wonder how on earth we managed without some of these devices and applications. I am heavily reliant on my mobile phone, and without the internet I would be lost – and not only because my business depends on it!

In the next part of this chapter I want to look a little more closely at a couple of the more modern ways we might choose to spend our leisure time – interacting on social media, and gaming.

How many 'friends' do I have?

I'm a relatively recent convert to social media. A number of years ago I joined Facebook because a friend was going to Australia for a year and it was a good way to stay in touch with her. I also discovered it was a good way to keep an eye on what my teenage sons were doing! It was quite enlightening to realise that I could learn more about what was going on in their lives through looking at their Facebook pages than they would actually tell me face to face! A couple of years ago I joined Twitter, too.

Social media is a great way to connect with people and to stay in touch with what is going on in people's lives. Teenagers in particular have embraced these tools with great enthusiasm. I read somewhere recently that only one per cent of Western teenagers don't use social networks. No sooner has something happened than they've tweeted about it, Snapchatted a photo or uploaded a picture to Facebook or Instagram for their cyberfriends to 'like' or comment on. But whatever generation we come from, we can have great fun seeing what our friends and family are getting up to, whether it's holiday snaps or a photograph of the hole in the ice in the town centre pond that they thought they could walk on (yes, my son did that).

Research has shown that social media benefits children and young people in a number of ways, including enhancing communication and technical skills, helping them to understand and cope with social norms, and enabling them to experiment with new forms of social expression. It also provides opportunities for extending their learning and for developing independence.[1]

Social media also offers great opportunities for people and businesses to network. Twitter, Facebook groups, sites such as LinkedIn and blogging enable people to market themselves and their businesses in very cost-effective ways.

I do wonder, though, how many people actually read what comes up on their timelines. Some people 'follow' thousands of accounts. If they were to read or even just glance at everything that was posted, surely they wouldn't have time to do anything else! I follow fewer than 300 people on Twitter, and I struggle to keep up with it! I have to be careful that it doesn't become a distraction and take up too much of my time that would be better spent doing more constructive things. That isn't to say that there is no value in what people post – of course there is; it is a great source of information, as well as some of the fun things that find their way on to it. But if I think about what I gain from social media in relation to how much time I spend on it, I sometimes think the time lost is bigger than the gains.

Social media is fun and a great tool, for adults and for young people, but it can easily become a hiding place. We choose carefully the image we want to present and the photographs we post, so that what people see is a carefully selected representation of us and our lives. How many 'selfies' do we take and delete before we finally take one that we're happy to post? How much goes on in our lives that we would be mortified to see posted for all to view?

Do we value ourselves or others by the number of friends or followers we have on these networks? Yet in reality, how many of these people could we really call true friends? How many of them could we count on in a crisis? How many could we call in the event of an emergency in the middle of the night and know they would come to our aid?

A while ago, I read an article entitled, 'Why Facebook makes you feel bad about yourself'. Research carried out by two German universities discovered that looking through photos posted by friends 'can trigger feelings of envy, misery and loneliness'. In a study of 600 people, one in three 'felt worse after visiting the site – especially if they viewed vacation photos'. Feelings of dissatisfaction can also arise from receiving fewer 'likes' or comments compared to friends.[2] And I'm sure we have all read some of the horror stories of the consequences of bullying on social media, and the dangers of chat rooms and of our children making 'friends' with people they don't know in real life.

I don't wish to portray social media entirely negatively. Indeed, it's a great way to keep in touch, to meet people with shared interests and a pleasant way to pass time. I just want to point out that, as with all things, we need to keep a careful balance, and to ensure that we have appropriate safety measures in place for our children.

Bringing the arcade home

Computer games are something I have never really been into. Back in the days of my youth (no, it wasn't that long ago!), Space Invaders, Pac-man and Super Mario were the games everyone seemed to be playing. I was always rubbish at them and usually chose not to play because I was so useless! On the odd occasion when the urge took hold of me, my terrible score would remind me why I never played such games!

Nowadays, arcade games have found their way into our living rooms and bedrooms via consoles, tablets, computers and phones. The graphics are very sophisticated, and the games are often very vivid. Again, they can be pleasant, harmless ways of passing time, and, as my son pointed out to me recently, they can be good for honing reaction times, skills of observation, strategic and creative thinking, decision-making skills and problem-solving ability. Some of the fitness games are good too, and promote staying active and interaction rather than spending too much time just sitting staring at screens.

Now that players are able to connect with each other via the internet, gaming offers opportunities to interact with friends. When I was a child we would play out in the street, even from a young age (I lived in a cul de sac so there were relatively few cars), but nowadays we don't feel that it is safe to allow our children out unsupervised. Gaming therefore offers an alternative way for them to play with their friends even when they are unable to be physically together. Recent reports have estimated that children aged three to four spend a little more than six hours per week playing games. This rises to more than nine hours for those between the ages of five and 15.[3]

However, as with all things, we need to be aware of some of the inherent dangers.

Addiction is one of these dangers. We can never win against these games – there is always someone with a higher score to beat or another level we need to pass, and instinctively we are driven to win. We just want to play one more level or reach a higher score before we go to bed, and just one more, and just one more... Lack of sleep because of game playing can have an adverse effect on our performance at work or at school. (Admittedly, this is a real temptation for book lovers too – just one more chapter...!)

There is also the effect that gaming can have on the social skills of young children. There is evidence that children who play games for three or more hours a day are less well-adjusted than those who have never played, or who play for less than an hour a day. However, the influence of video games was found to be smaller than that of family function, material deprivation and school.[4]

Research has also suggested that regular action gaming can reduce activity in the hippocampus – the part of the brain that is responsible for memory and spatial awareness. Lack of activity in this area of the brain can precede mental disorders such as Alzheimer's disease.[5]

One of the other dangers is the distance these games have from reality. I am sure that for most people this is not a problem, as most of us are fully aware that in real life, if someone dies, they stay dead; they don't get up again and rejoin the game. Yet I can't help thinking that the violence we see in games, in films and in the media in general – even what is reported on the news – has something to do with the seeming increase in violent crime over recent years. Am I the only one who thinks that games, films and television programmes can put ideas into the minds of people who might perhaps be pushed off balance without too much effort? Am I alone in thinking that the graphic reporting of crime in the media can give ideas for 'copycat' crimes to other would-be criminals?

What about Jesus?

Obviously, the problems raised by social media and computer games were not issues that Jesus and His followers ever faced. We looked in chapter 7 at some of the ways Jesus passed His time and the things He focused His attention on, so I won't cover these again.

However, I would like to leave you with just one thought: if social media had been around in Jesus' day, I wonder what kinds of things He would have posted. Would He have posted selfies of Him and His disciples chilling out at the home of Mary, Martha and Lazarus, or having breakfast on the beach? Why not? Jesus enjoyed having fun and He knew the importance of relaxation, and I don't see any reason why He would not have promoted some R & R time occasionally.

Would Jesus have used the sites as tools to promote Himself, or might He have found creative ways to use them as a means of bringing healing, restoration and reconciliation? Perhaps He would have tweeted some of His most famous sayings, such as, 'Do to others as you would have them do to you' (Luke 6:31). What might Jesus' reaction be to some of the things we post?

The challenge for us is, how will we use social media to spread the good news of the kingdom of God? I'm not suggesting that we never post selfies, or that we never have fun with social media. I strongly believe God is the originator and creator of fun, and that He loves to see His children having a laugh and enjoying themselves. We just need to be aware of the potential impact of some of the things we post, and do our best to ensure that others will be encouraged, enlightened and inspired, and not be left feeling inadequate or lacking in any way by the things we put on our timelines.

Notes

[1] Ito Mizuko et al, University of California, 'Living and Learning with New Media: Summary of Findings from the Digital Youth Project', November 2008. Available at http://digitalyouth.ischool.berkeley.edu/files/report/digitalyouth-TwoPageSummary.pdf (accessed 11th June 2015).
[2] Alexandra Sifferlin, 'Why Facebook makes you feel bad about yourself', *Time*, 24th January 2013. Available at http://healthland.time.com/2013/01/24/why-facebook-makes-you-feel-bad-about-yourself/?iid=hl-article-mostpop1 (accessed 24th July 2014).
[3] Dr Bex Lewis, 'Little Gamers', *Childrenswork*, June 2015. Available at http://www.premierchildrenswork.com/Past-Issues/2015/June-July-2015/Little-Gamers (accessed 12th June 2015).
[4] Research by Oxford University's Internet Institute, 2014. Cited in Lewis, 'Little Gamers'.
[5] Chris Green, 'Playing action-based video games could make you more prone to mental disorders, study claims', *The Independent*, 2nd May 2015. Available at http://www.independent.co.uk/life-style/health-and-families/health-news/playing-actionbased-video-games-could-make-you-more-prone-to-mental-disorders-study-claims-10261295.html (accessed 12th June 2015).

Chapter 11
It's easy to say, but...

[Jesus] took the blind man by the hand and led him
out of the village.'
Mark 8:23

We have talked about some of the places where we might hide, and we have looked at the model of Jesus and how He lived on earth without hiding. It's easy to say, 'Let's step out of our hiding places,' but how do we do it? What does it look like, in practical terms?

As I mentioned in the introduction, we often invite Jesus into our hiding places with us. We want a relationship with Him, but we are frightened to step out with Him. We don't want to upset the status quo and we certainly don't want to feel we will have to make changes in our lives. So we make a counter-offer to Jesus. He offers us freedom, hope, joy, peace, blessing, and so many other things besides. We pick and choose what we want, based on what we think it might cost us.

God is so gracious. His love for us is so big that He will join us where we are, in our pokey little hidey-hole among the trees, where we feel safe and comfortable with the familiar. But He doesn't want to stay there with us. All the time He is longing to take us by the hand and lead us out into the fresh air, into the wide open space where we will be free to express ourselves, to dance, to sing, to write, to draw, to paint, to cook, to laugh, to talk, to build, to do so many things that we cannot do effectively in the cramped darkness. But He will never impose Himself on us. His hand is always extended to us, waiting; but He will never force us to do anything we don't want to do.

In Mark 8:23, quoted at the beginning of this chapter, Jesus took the blind man by the hand and led him out of the village. Then He healed him. Would Jesus have healed him if they had stayed in the village? Was it necessary for them to leave the village in order for the man to receiving his healing? I don't know. But perhaps he needed to take this step of faith in order to receive the gift that Jesus wanted to give him. Maybe it was too crowded in the village; perhaps it was too noisy; or maybe it was the wrong environment for the man to see for the first time. Whatever the motivation, we can be sure that Jesus knew exactly what He was doing, and He had very good reasons for leading the man out before healing him.

Maybe that is how it is for us too, sometimes. Maybe the environment we are in is not conducive to our healing. Maybe it is important for our own faith and relationship with Jesus to take a step of faith before we receive what He longs to give us. The initial step of faith very often is a part of the healing process, as we learn to trust and relinquish some of the control we desperately want to hang on to. As we step out with Him, we are able to receive what He wants to give us, and can begin to embrace the life He has planned for us, and continue to be transformed into His image and according to His likeness, and to follow the path He wants to walk with us. Rest assured that He will never leave you to walk the path alone. Once you take hold of His hand, He will never let you go.

So what does it look like, to step out of our hiding places, to embrace the freedom that is being offered to us?

I'd like to offer here a few of my observations, and to talk about some of my own experiences as to what it has looked like for me. Let me add here that I am not an expert, and for all that I am coming out of my hiding places and letting go of my fig leaves, I am very aware that there are still times and areas where I struggle. I am still very much a work in progress and on my own journey, but I hope my experiences and observations might be helpful to some, even just as a starting point.

Consider your heart

One of the things I have always maintained is that if our heart is truly after God, He won't allow us to go too far wrong. That isn't to say, of course, that we won't make mistakes. But I do believe that if we earnestly and truly desire to serve God, He will keep us on His path.

As I have said before, God knows us intimately, better than we know ourselves. He knows our true motivations, our heart's desires, our passions, our needs – indeed, everything about us. We don't always even know these things ourselves, and we are so often confused about how we feel and what we should do. But if our number one priority in everything we do is to please and serve God, He will grant us our heart's desire.

When our heart is truly after God, He puts on our hearts the things He wants us to be passionate about. I guess this goes back to taking on the characteristics of our parents – and of our heavenly Father, as we spend more and more time with Him and grow into a deeper relationship with Him.

God's heart is infinite, and it is big enough to hold all the needs and desires of the world. Our hearts are much smaller, but they still have an immense capacity for love, for justice, for compassion, for kindness and generosity, and for all those qualities that God is, just on a smaller scale. As God shares His passions with us, He puts on our hearts the things that He wants us to do something about. That might be to pray, to offer financial support to a particular cause, to be a voice for the voiceless, or to be more actively involved. God's heart is big enough to hold all the causes of the world, and He shares them out so that between all of His children, they are all covered. No one person can change the world, but we can all make a difference in our little corner of it. Along with the passion, God gives opportunities.

I realise this is quite a simplistic way of looking at it, and I am certainly not suggesting that we focus on one or two things to the exclusion of everything else. We have a responsibility, as God's children, to speak up wherever we see injustice, and to offer help whenever we can. We must not sit back and let something go, just because it doesn't fall into the area that we believe God has put on our heart.

Sometimes our passions come as a sudden revelation; at other times they creep up on us gradually. But it is important to listen to our hearts, and to follow the desires that God gives us.

A few years ago I was suddenly struck by the desire to go to Bible college. It was almost as if it slapped me round the face, it was so sudden! It came as quite a shock to me. It was the last thing I expected that God would want me to do.

I spent the next few weeks praying about it, talking to my husband and children (obviously it would have an impact on them so it was important to involve them in the decision), and talking to other Christians I love and respect. I began to recognise that studying Theology was something I would always have loved to do, had I allowed myself to want it. My circumstances up until that point had meant that it would not have been possible, so it had never even entered my head as an option for me.

But now my circumstances were such that the course which had come to my attention – an undergraduate degree in Kingdom Theology with the Westminster Theological Centre – might actually be practically possible for me to do. When I had left my part-time job a few months earlier, I had had a feeling that God had something else in mind for me to do, but I had no idea what it might be.

As I prayed over this decision, I actually didn't feel that God was saying anything at all. I was hoping for a big YES to write itself across the sky, but it didn't happen! There was silence. But on the basis that God wasn't saying 'No' either, I decided to pursue it and see what would happen, all the time praying hard that God would close the door if it wasn't a path He wanted me to follow.

One of the biggest hurdles was the timing of the first study residential. My husband and I had been blessed with the gift of a few days' holiday at the end of August, and I was also going to a three-day conference in early September, and I knew that the course residentials always take place towards the end of August/early September. The dates fitted perfectly – the residential fitted neatly between our holiday and the conference.

So on the basis that God still wasn't closing the door, I went ahead and applied to do the course. All the time I was praying for God to make it clear what He wanted me to do. This was a big decision – I was potentially committing the next six years of my life, and I knew that to take on something so big if God wasn't in it would be a big mistake. Yet, even though I still wasn't hearing a definite yes, I wasn't hearing a no either.

Looking back, I believe God had put the passion on my heart to pursue this course. It was as though a carrot had been dangled, and even though it had never been there before and I had therefore never missed it, now I had seen it, I really wanted it.

I was accepted on the course and started a few weeks later. Once I had committed to it, God very graciously and clearly confirmed that this was the right path for me, and I have to say that the course is a tremendous blessing, and I am loving it! It isn't easy – it stretches me and challenges me, and raises as many questions as it brings answers – but I am enjoying it immensely and learning so much. And when I say it is a 'blessing' – I mean it comes with a responsibility to use what I am gaining too. I have opportunities to preach, to teach and to write, and God is able to use what I am learning – I hope – to bless others as well.

So if our hearts are truly for God, and we earnestly desire to be obedient to Him, I believe He will give us desires to do things that might even surprise us. As we do these things, He can use them to lead us out of some of our hiding places.

Awareness

God might make us aware of things that He wants to change in us. It might not be obvious at first that it is a 'hiding place', but God wants the best for us, and He works in us in lots of different ways. The hiding places we use are not limited to the things I have mentioned in this book: anything that gets in the way of our relationship with Him is a tree behind which we are hiding; anything that gets in the way of our relationships with others is a fig leaf we are attempting to clothe ourself with.

As I have already mentioned, God is gentle, and deals with each of us according to our own personality, background, experiences and needs. If we are becoming aware of something in our life that doesn't feel quite right, if there is something we feel uncomfortable about, we should bring it to God in prayer and ask Him what He wants us to do.

It might be something that we find difficult to let go of; in that case we need to ask Him for His help. I spoke earlier of a controlling relationship that I was once involved in. Once I was free of this relationship, God was able to repair the damage that had been done. However, one thing I knew I needed to do was to forgive. That wasn't easy, but I gradually realised that if I didn't forgive, the only person who would be affected would be me, as I held on to anger and resentment and allowed it to take root. I confess it wasn't something I wanted to do, and I had to ask God not only to help me to forgive, but also to make me willing to forgive and let go.

It wasn't an overnight process – and for a long time things still came back to haunt me, and I found myself having to make a conscious decision to let them go – but as time went on it gradually became easier. As God made me aware of this hiding place, and as I asked Him to help me, He enabled me to begin to step out.

Prayer and the word of God

Perhaps this is the most obvious of all. Prayer is one of the ways we sustain our relationship with God, and it is, as we all know, a two-way process. Through prayer we give God the opportunity to speak to us, and as we spend time with Him, we are able to adopt more of His habits and characteristics. Reading the Bible is also important, as we learn about our Father and His Big Plan for humankind, and as we begin to scrape the surface of the whole Salvation Story. God is able to speak to us through His word, too, and as we spend more and more time with Him, we are better able to recognise His voice whenever He speaks to us. As we spend time with Him and His word, He will continue to transform us into His image and according to His likeness.

As I look back over recent years, I realise that stepping out of some of my hiding places is not something I could ever have done alone. In some ways it is almost something that 'happened' to me. God changes us from the inside, and sometimes there isn't much we can do to help the process, other than be willing to be changed.

That isn't to say, of course, that we become passive recipients, like baby birds in the nest who sit with their mouths open waiting to be fed. Perhaps there are times when we need to be like that, but sooner or later the baby birds need to learn to fly. We need to be praying, seeking God's will and His heart for us, examining our hearts and our lives with reference to God's word and seeing where He might want to make changes in us and in our lives, and lead us forward.

Community

I have talked about how God created us to be relational beings. We are not meant to be alone. Community with God's people is very important, and it is vital that we consciously and deliberately have people around us who not only love us for who God has made us to be, but who will also be honest with us.

Accountability is crucial if we are to move forward. We need relationships with one or two people – it doesn't have to be many – who we know will be completely honest with us, including about our weaknesses and our mistakes. These must be people with whom we know we are secure, and the relationships must be built on a foundation of love and trust. Without that secure base, the relationship will not be strong enough to withstand what might sometimes be hard truths that need to be spoken.

Pick wisely. Choose people who you know are godly, prayerful people. You might want to put in place a formal accountability relationship, such as a mentoring relationship or a prayer partnership, or it might be a natural relationship you already have with a close friend or your partner. People who know us well and who are able to be honest with us can sometimes see more objectively some of the places where we hide. But these people will also be honest with us about our strengths, and will encourage us and speak words of praise when they are needed, too.

No relationship is perfect. We all make mistakes, and there will inevitably be times when one of us says the wrong thing, or uses inappropriate words, or when the timing is bad, or even when things that are said are misinterpreted. This is why the solid foundation is crucial. At times like this it is vital to talk about the issue and how it made us feel, so that we can resolve it and put it behind us.

I remember an occasion when someone, completely unintentionally, said something to me that I found a little upsetting. I didn't take it personally, however, as I knew that they were particularly passionate about the subject and had allowed their emotions to take over. This person was made aware, by a third party, that what they had said was out of order, so they apologised to me and asked my forgiveness. I was very tempted to say, 'It's fine, don't worry, you didn't upset me – there's nothing to forgive.' But I recognised that, actually, that wouldn't be honest, and in the long run it wouldn't be helpful to the other person either. So I chose my words carefully and said that yes, I had been a little upset by their words, but I understood their reasons for what they had said, and yes, of course I forgave them.

I am so grateful for the people God has put around me to love me and be honest with me. There are times when I don't like what I hear, but because I know and respect these people, I will go away and think and pray about what has been said. Sometimes I might come to the conclusion that I don't agree, and that's fine – they won't always be right. But often they are right, and I am very grateful that they love me enough to be honest with me.

Step out of the zone

Hiding places are, by nature, comfortable. They are warm, cosy and familiar. Stepping out into the cold, where we feel exposed and vulnerable, can be incredibly difficult. But there comes a time when the baby birds must learn how to fly. They cannot spend the rest of their lives in the nest, passively being fed, because that is not what they were made for. Birds were made to fly, and sooner or later they have to jump out of the nest and hope their wings will carry them!

But they don't do it on their own. The mother bird is always there to show them what to do, to guide them and to help them. Their ability to fly is God given, and only when they take that step will they find that they can do it! They might fall flat on their faces, but they pick themselves up and try again – and sooner or later, they get it!

In the same way, we need to find our wings. God has given us abilities and gifts, and we cannot stay in the nest for ever, otherwise our gifts and abilities will be wasted. When the time is right, God, our mother bird, will show us how to fly. We may fall once or twice, but that's OK – God will pick us up and we will have another go. And what a feeling it is when we achieve it!

The first time I preached a sermon, I felt that I was way out of my comfort zone! As someone who has always been painfully shy and fearful of what other people think of me, I felt very exposed and vulnerable. What if I were to make a fool of myself? What if I were to fall over my words? What if I were to get stage fright and couldn't open my mouth?! But I felt it was what God was asking me to do, and He had given me a message to share, so I did everything that was humanly possible in terms of preparation, research, practice and so on, and trusted Him for the rest. As I sat in the congregation during the service, my palms were sweaty, my stomach was turning somersaults and I found it hard to concentrate on what was going on, but God met me as I stepped out, and once I got going, I found I really enjoyed myself! I received positive feedback and have been invited to preach a number of times since, so I guess the message must have come across reasonably well, too!

As we offer our five small loaves and two tiny fish, God is able to take our offering and multiply it. As we step out from behind our trees, God is right there, holding our hand and walking with us every step of the way.

Chapter 12
Complete, but not yet fulfilled

Our Father in heaven,
hallowed be your name.
Your kingdom come.
Your will be done,
on earth as it is in heaven.
Matthew 6:9-10

We have spent some time exploring how we are made in the image and according to the likeness of God, and we have looked at the consequences of the Fall of humankind. We have seen how Adam and Eve hid from God and from each other as a result of their shame; we have examined some of the common hiding places that we use in the twenty-first century and ways God can help us to step out of those hiding places. We have considered how Jesus lived on earth and looked at the example He gave us by living without hiding.

We saw in chapter 3 that God put in place a Rescue Plan to save humanity from the consequences of their sin. I want to spend a little time in this chapter looking at this Plan and how God wants us to be a part of that Plan.

When Adam and Eve ate of the fruit of the forbidden tree, their lives and the world as they knew it changed almost beyond recognition. As we saw earlier, they had to leave the garden, and they had to live with the serious consequences of their actions, including the distortion of the image of God in humankind. God dealt with the immediate problem and made clothes out of animal skins for them, and began to put in place His long-term Rescue Plan.

This Rescue Plan could not be carried out overnight. It took thousands of years to bring it to fruition, and along the way it involved covenants with Noah, with the family of Abraham and with the nation of Israel, and it culminated in the new covenant in Jesus, the second Adam.

The first Adam was created without sin, in a perfect, uncorrupted world, and he gave in to temptation. The second Adam was born into a corrupt, sinful world but He overcame the power of sin and lived a perfect life. He, too, faced temptations, but He resisted them. Through one man and one woman, sin entered the world, and the consequences were death for every human being. But God's love for His children was far stronger than the power of death, and through one man, the God-man, the curse of sin was vanquished and death was defeated, once and for all:

> For since death came through a human being, the resurrection of the dead has also come through a human being; for as all die in Adam, so all will be made alive in Christ.
> *1 Corinthians 15:21-22*

Jesus took upon Himself the consequences that each one of us should ultimately have borne. God said quite clearly that the consequences of eating of the fruit of the tree were that the one who ate of it would die (Genesis 2:17). But because He loves us so much, God could not allow this to happen, so God chose to become flesh in the form of Jesus – fully divine and fully human – to suffer this death in our place, so that the eternal life humanity had been created to enjoy could be restored to us. Paul tells us:

> Therefore just as one man's trespass led to condemnation for all, so one man's act of righteousness

leads to justification and life for all. For just as by the one man's disobedience the many were made sinners, so by the one man's obedience the many will be made righteous.
Romans 5:18-19

On the cross, Jesus took the consequences of our sin, the curse that should have been borne by us. The consequences of death, sickness and decay, pain, fear, sadness, broken relationships, daily struggles, and everything else that was brought upon humanity at the Fall, were all placed on Jesus at the cross, so that in the fullness of time, we could live in eternity, free from them all. Isaiah tells us:

Surely he has borne our infirmities
and carried our diseases;
yet we accounted him stricken,
struck down by God, and afflicted.
But he was wounded for our transgressions;
crushed for our iniquities;
upon him was the punishment that made us whole,
and by his bruises we are healed.
All we like sheep have gone astray;
we have all turned to our own way,
and the Lord has laid on him
the iniquity of us all.
Isaiah 53:4-6

Through Jesus, God's original plan of life in a perfect world can now be a reality for us all. The Rescue Plan was completed when Jesus died and rose again from the dead, although it has not yet been brought to fruition. Christ has taken the consequences of humanity's sin – the physical, spiritual and relational consequences – and has destroyed the curse of death.

It is complete, and we are awaiting its fulfilment at the end of time, when Jesus will return and take us to be with Himself.

In chapters 21 and 22 of the book of Revelation we are given a glimpse of what the fulfilment of the Plan will look like. The first heaven and earth will pass away, and the new heaven and the new earth will come 'down out of heaven from God, prepared as a bride adorned for her husband' (Revelation 21:1-2). This new heaven and new earth, to my mind, will bear a remarkable resemblance to the Garden of Eden:

> 'See, the home of God is among mortals.
> He will dwell with them;
> they will be his peoples,
> and God himself will be with them;
> he will wipe every tear from their eyes.
> Death will be no more;
> mourning and crying and pain will be no more,
> for the first things have passed away.'
> *Revelation 21:3-4*

> I saw no temple in the city, for its temple is the Lord God the Almighty and the Lamb. And the city has no need of sun or moon to shine on it, for the glory of God is its light, and its lamp is the Lamb.
> *Revelation 21:22-23*

> Then the angel showed me the river of the water of life, bright as crystal, flowing from the throne of God and of the Lamb through the middle of the street of the city. On either side of the river is the tree of life with its twelve kinds of fruit, producing its fruit each month; and the leaves of the tree are for the healing of the nations. Nothing accursed will be found there any more. But the throne of God and of the Lamb will be in it, and his servants will worship him; they will see his

face, and his name will be on their foreheads. And there will be no more night; they will need no light of lamp or sun, for the Lord God will be their light, and they will reign for ever and ever.
Revelation 22:1-5

We are also told in Scripture that we will undergo a physical transformation at that time, and that our bodies will be changed to resemble the body of the risen Lord Jesus:

But our citizenship is in heaven, and it is from there that we are expecting a Saviour, the Lord Jesus Christ. He will transform the body of our humiliation so that it may be conformed to the body of his glory, by the power that also enables him to make all things subject to himself.
Philippians 3:20-21

At the moment of our salvation we are given eternal life, and at the fulfilment of the Plan, our bodies will be transformed so that they once again fully reflect the glorious image and likeness of God.

So what do we do in the meantime, while we are waiting for the fulfilment of God's Plan? Do we just sit back and kill time, twiddling our thumbs and waiting for the return of Jesus? Jesus made it quite clear that He wants all people to be restored to Him, and He commissioned the disciples, and all of His followers, to 'Go therefore and make disciples of all nations' (Matthew 28:19). Let us note that He said 'Go'; He didn't say, 'Sit in your church buildings and wait for people to come to you.' Peter in his letter reminds us of God's desire for *all* people to be restored to Him:

> The Lord is not slow about his promise, as some think
> of slowness, but is patient with you, not wanting any to
> perish, but all to come to repentance.
> *2 Peter 3:9*

As we wait for the fulfilment of God's Rescue Plan, we need to play an active part in the rescue party, and go out to save others. God has a different job for each of us to do; we each have our own part to play in this Rescue Plan, and He will equip us with whatever we need to do it. He offers us gifts to equip us, to help us do the job He has given us. Let us receive these gifts He is offering to us – remember, He won't force them on us if we choose not to accept them – so that we can fulfil our part of His Plan.

We are each called to play a different role in the Plan, but each part is vitally important. We are all called by God to full-time Christian ministry in a particular role, whether we work for a church or a Christian organisation or in a secular environment. Some are called to be evangelists, and seem to be equipped with a special ability to tell people about Jesus. I look at some of these people sometimes and know that they are gifted, because I certainly am unable to speak to people in the way they can! But I also know that God has gifted me in different ways, and I must play the part God has called me to. Some might be able to give financially; others might be called to be full-time missionaries; still others are called to be 'prayer warriors'.

No matter what our calling, though, we are all called to have a voice and to stand up for what we believe in. We can all make our views heard in a number of different ways – perhaps through the use of social media, through lobbying our local council or member of Parliament. We can write to companies that we believe use unethical practices, and vote with our feet. One day we will be called to give an account of the way we have lived, and we will be judged accordingly. Will I have done everything I can to tell others the good news, to make a positive difference in the lives of as many as possible?

The image and likeness of God in human beings was badly damaged, but, thanks to God's Rescue Plan, it was not destroyed. Human beings still reflect God's image, no matter who they are or how 'bad' we think they might be. We are to respect all people, created as they have been in His image, no matter who they are or what they have done. Jesus reminded us:

> '"For I was hungry and you gave me food, I was thirsty and you gave me something to drink, I was a stranger and you welcomed me, I was naked and you gave me clothing, I was sick and you took care of me, I was in prison and you visited me." Then the righteous will answer him, "Lord, when was it that we saw you hungry and gave you food, or thirsty and gave you something to drink? And when was it that we saw you a stranger and welcomed you, or naked and gave you clothing? And when was it that we saw you sick or in prison and visited you?" And the king will answer them, "Truly I tell you, just as you did it to one of the least of these who are members of my family, you did it to me."'
> *Matthew 25:35-40*

As we draw closer to Him and become more like Him, God is working to restore His image in each one of us. We are called to be His agents in the world, to work with Him to draw people back to Him so that they too can be rescued and fulfil their part in His Plan.

God's Spirit is on the move, reviving His church and awakening His people. He longs to shower His Spirit upon us, equipping and enabling us, and we should be hungry for more of Him and His gifts.

I have just returned from the New Wine Christian Conference in Shepton Mallet in Somerset. During one of the evening meetings, there was a time of quiet during which we were invited to offer our own personal worship to God. For a while it was quiet, and then gradually people began to speak and sing, some in English, some in tongues.[1] It was such a beautiful sound, so gentle and pure – almost angelic. As I listened to this and offered my own words of worship to God, I received a picture in my mind of a cloud of God's presence hovering over the people at one side of the arena. As I watched, the cloud gradually unrolled all the way across the arena, and then God's blessing fell like drops of rain on to the people below, ready to soak those who were willing to receive it.

God longs to bless His people, to equip us to go out and serve Him. But let's remember that His blessings and gifts are not to be received purely for our own benefit. They come with a job to do, and we have a responsibility not to keep them for ourselves but to use them in His service.

God does not wait for us to reach a certain standard of perfection, or even goodness, before He uses us. He takes us just as we are and is able to use us, in spite of our shortcomings, to bring about His plans. Somebody once said (and I'm afraid I don't know who it was), 'God loves me just the way I am, but He loves me too much to leave me the way I am.' That pretty much sums it up, really!

We are all works in progress – and I know that I for one have a long way to go. Yet I know that God *is* working in me, and He is transforming me, bit by bit, day by day.

In Colossians, Paul says:

> You have stripped off the old self with its practices and have clothed yourselves with the new self, which is being renewed in knowledge according to the image of its creator. … As God's chosen ones, holy and beloved,

clothe yourselves with compassion, kindness, humility, meekness, and patience. Bear with one another and, if anyone has a complaint against another, forgive each other; just as the Lord has forgiven you, so you also must forgive. Above all, clothe yourselves with love, which binds everything together in perfect harmony.
Colossians 3:9-10, 12-14

This analogy of putting on new clothes to me is a reminder of the clothing God fashioned for Adam and Eve before they left the garden – clothing He knew they would need to equip them and protect them as they faced their new circumstances. As we are being 'renewed in knowledge according to the image of [our] creator', He clothes us, too, with the garments we need to equip us for and to protect us in our own particular circumstances.

Paul then goes on to list the 'clothing' that we are to put on, the 'garments' that God provides for us: compassionate hearts, kindness, humility, meekness, patience, forbearance, forgiveness, and above all, love. These are the qualities of our heavenly Father, and as we spend time with Him and allow Him to transform us, they are the qualities we will adopt and begin to reflect, too, as His image and likeness in us are gradually restored.

God will help us to come out of our hiding places and will enable us to take hold of the plans He has for our lives. I'm sure many of us are using multiple hiding places, but let us be assured that God doesn't expect us to emerge from them all at once. He takes us by the hand and helps us to come out, step by step, little by little, as much as we can cope with at a time. He works on us gently and gradually, transforming and renewing us, and restoring His image in us, one day at a time.

And all of us, with unveiled faces, seeing the glory of the Lord as though reflected in a mirror, are being transformed into the same image from one degree of glory to another; for this comes from the Lord, the Spirit.

2 Corinthians 3:18

Notes

[1] For an explanation of 'speaking in tongues', see Acts 2:1-4.

Epilogue

I'd like to finish with a picture that God gave to me a while ago. It's a beautiful picture, and I hope it will leave you with a taster of what is to come, of the treasure He has in store for us all, and May it help us all to remember just how much He loves each one of us.

The invitation

Let me take you on a little trip.

One day, you receive an invitation to a huge banquet. The invitation is beautifully decorated and very personal to you. It's just for you. It makes you feel special and loved, even though you're not even sure who it's from.

You check the date in your diary and accept the invitation.

As the time for the banquet draws nearer you start to prepare for it. It's a very important occasion so you'll need something special to wear. You go shopping and take time choosing the perfect outfit – dress, shoes, bag, accessories; or suit, shirt, tie, shoes. You really want to look your best.

When the day comes, you might go to the hairdresser's or the barber's and have your hair done. You might even have a manicure (ladies, that is…). You'll take your time getting ready – you'll have a shower and get dressed slowly to make sure your outfit looks as good as it can be. Guys, you'll have a shave; girls, you'll take time applying your make-up.

You don't have to worry about how you'll get there. The invitation tells you that a car will come to collect you at 7.00pm. You make sure you're ready in good time, and at 7.00 sharp the doorbell rings. The driver greets you warmly and opens the door for you to step into the car. You don't really understand why, but you're being made to feel as though you're an honoured guest at this banquet.

Finally you arrive at the location where the banquet is being held. You're feeling apprehensive. You still don't really know why you've been invited, but you do know that something compelled you to accept the invitation and to come along. Something inside tells you this is a big deal, that you just had to be here. Your palms start to get a bit sweaty. You have butterflies in your stomach – you don't even know how you're going to manage to eat anything, you feel so nervous. Will you even know anyone there?

How are you going to make your entrance? Will you just go in? Will you be met at the door? Will you be able to slip in quietly, unobtrusively, without making a big fuss in front of a lot of people?

The driver opens the car door for you and walks you to the door of the house. His smile is somehow reassuring, although your nerves are still there.

Your heart is pounding. You take a deep breath and knock gently at the door. Immediately it is flung wide open. Your host comes out and throws His arms around you. 'I'm so glad you've arrived!' He says with a huge grin on His face. 'We've been waiting for you. Come in, come in.'

You're feeling more than a little surprised. Has He got the right person? Has He mistaken you for someone else? You know you certainly don't deserve such a welcome. You don't know whether to feel pleased at being welcomed so warmly, or even more worried that perhaps He sent the invitation to the wrong person. Was the invitation meant for someone else? Are you even meant to be here?

You hang back, wondering whether or not to follow Him. He stops, turns round and looks you straight in the eye. 'Don't be nervous,' He says. 'The invitation *was* meant for you. I haven't mistaken you for someone else. I've been waiting for you for years. I know exactly who you are, and I know everything about you – yes, everything. I love you so much, and I went to an awful lot of trouble to bring you here. You belong here, and I'm so glad you've finally arrived.'

He takes you by the hand and walks by your side along a hallway. It's beautiful, and very peaceful. You can see a large door at the end of the corridor, and as you approach you begin to hear noises coming from the other side. It sounds like a party, and whoever is there is having a great time!

You come to the door. He pauses and looks you straight in the eye again. 'Ready?' He asks.

'I'm not sure,' you reply. 'I don't know what to expect.'

'Just trust Me,' He says. 'We're going to have a ball! This is a day of great celebration!'

He opens the door and leads you in, still holding your hand. You gasp at the sight in front of you. It's a huge banqueting hall, the like of which you've never seen in your life. It's absolutely amazing. The walls are made of precious stones, and it's drenched in bright sunshine, like a beautiful garden in the summer. The room is full of exquisitely decorated tables, and people are sitting at the tables.

Running through the middle of the hall, just near you, is a river. The water is clearer and purer than any water you've ever seen, and somehow you just know that it is life-giving water. It will refresh you in a way you've never been refreshed before, and fill you with all the energy and vitality you need, for ever.

At the far end of the hall you can see a huge throne, and on it you can just make out a figure. You can't see Him properly because so much light is emanating from Him that you have to shield your eyes – He is the source of the light. To the side of this throne is another throne, but it's empty, and you just know that the one holding your hand is the one who should be sitting there.

That's His rightful place, yet He stepped down from His throne because He's so excited about your arrival and He just had to come and welcome you personally.

You're still trying to take all of this in and make sense of it all when you become aware of voices calling your name. You look around at the people sitting at the tables. They're laughing and joking together. They're singing to the figure on the throne. They're eating and enjoying the delicious food. Somehow – and you don't really know quite how – they're doing all three at once!

You realise that not every seat at the tables is filled – there must be more guests due to arrive. As you look around the hall you see your friends and family. They are calling you and waving to you. You can see from the look on their faces that they're very excited to see you.

You wave back, tentatively, still not completely sure what's going on. Your host leads you to a vacant place at a table and says to you, 'Here's your place. I've been saving it for you.' You look, and there's an empty seat where the table is laid ready, and it's labelled with your name. He draws the chair out for you – an ornate, throne-like chair – and invites you to take your place.

He smiles at you. He smiles with His whole face, particularly His eyes. It's a smile that says to you, 'You're so very special. I've been waiting so long for this moment and I'm so excited that it's finally arrived. I love you so much.'

It all begins to fall into place. He's been waiting for me. He loves me so much. He's kept this place for me – a place at His table. He left His throne because He wanted to welcome me personally. I don't deserve this, yet I belong here. This is my home.

He smiles even more broadly as He sees that you are now beginning to understand. He gently pushes your chair in towards the table and kisses you on the top of your head. 'Please excuse me. Another of my guests is arriving and I want to welcome them.'

You take a deep breath and look around you once more. Your friends and family realise you need a moment and they give you some breathing space – they needed it too when they first arrived. You look towards the figure on the throne. 'Thank You,' you whisper in your heart. 'I know I don't deserve this, but thank You.'

'You're welcome,' you hear a voice reply. It's not an audible voice; you hear it in your heart. 'As I said to you just now, I went to a lot of trouble to bring you here, and I'm so glad you accepted my invitation. I love you.'

'I love You too,' you say in return, and you mean it in a way you've never meant it before. There's a new depth to your love that you've never been able to experience and express before.

You smile, and sit quietly for a few minutes, trying to take it all in. Then you turn to those around you. They're looking at you, and they have the biggest smiles on their faces. They know exactly what's going on in your heart and in your mind, because they're feeling it too. They felt it when they first arrived, and they're still feeling it now – the feeling never goes away. It's a joy beyond understanding, a peace that cannot be defined, and a love that is deeper than any love that can ever be felt.

You smile at them. 'Hi,' you say. 'I'm home.'

They feast on the abundance of your house,
and you give them drink from the river of your
delights.
For with you is the fountain of life;
in your light we see light.
Psalm 36:8-9

Also by Nicki Copeland

'Nicki ... demonstrates her courage in facing some of the aspects of her personality that once hindered her and would have continued to do so had she not first faced them and then braved writing about them here.'
Lindsay Melluish, Regional Leader, New Wine London & South East; Associate Pastor, St Paul's Ealing

Every one of us is born with great potential. Our life experiences, personality and self-opinions shape who we become, and what we do with that potential. Some seem to effortlessly soar, while others are left grounded and feeling distinctly 'less than ordinary'.

Having struggled for much of her life with low self-esteem and lack of confidence, Nicki Copeland shares her personal journey into self-acceptance and growing belief in herself. She talks openly and honestly about some of the highs and lows of her life, and how she has begun to blossom into the person she has been uniquely created to be.

'Easy to read, honest and thoughtful ... Many women will relate to Nicki's feelings, and this book is a real encouragement to all.' *Gill, physiotherapist*

'It will build up your heart and help you learn to love yourself.' *Caroline, full-time mum*

'This book is refreshingly honest and offers practical advice and wisdom.' *Helen, charity accountant*

'Nicki's story has deeply moved me.' *Clare, church ministry leader*

Published by Instant Apostle. ISBN 978-1-909728-00-4. RRP £7.99